ADVANCED
Dressage Training
Medium to Grand Prix

ADVANCED
Dressage Training
Medium to Grand Prix

Angela Niemeyer Eastwood
with Andrea Hessay

THE CROWOOD PRESS

First published in 2015 by
The Crowood Press Ltd
Ramsbury, Marlborough
Wiltshire SN8 2HR

www.crowood.com

British Library Cataloguing-in-Publication Data
A catalogue record for this book is available from the British Library.

ISBN 978 1 78500 088 1

Frontispiece: Legs in the air – not a classic move but shows good elevation! (Photo: Andrew Griffin)

Dedication
To all the horses we have known – thank you.

Every science and every art has its principles and its rules that lead to new discoveries and to perfection. Why should horsemanship be the only art for which practice alone is needed?

de la Guérinière (École de Cavalerie 1733)

Typeset by Jean Cussons Typesetting, Diss, Norfolk

Printed and bound in Malaysia by Times Offset (M) Sdn Bhd

Contents

Acknowledgements

Acknowledgements and thanks are due to the following:

The Talland team – Pammy, Pippa, Charlie, Abi and their staff – for their co-operation, time, effort and support.

Hayley Watson-Greaves.

Team Talland, left to right: AEH; Abi and Charlie Hutton; Pammy and Pippa Hutton; ANE.

To Team Pincus, their staff and horses at Sheepcote, for their time, effort and consideration in helping to make the chapter 'Work In-Hand' worthwhile. Details and a biography are given at the end of the book.

The owners of Pepe, Sam, Amo, Magnum, Duela, Polly. Details and a biography of Talland are given at the end of the book.

The same degree of thanks is due to Hayley Watson-Greaves and her lovely horse WG Rubins Nite for a similar level of co-operation and support. Details and a biography are given at the end of the book.

Sheepcote: AEH; David Pincus; ANE.

To Sarah Pook for several photographs, taken by photography student, Oonagh McGibbon, at Sarah's home in Hampshire during one of Angela's clinics there.

Kevin Sparrow, official photographer at London 2012.

Sarah Pook and Top Pride, ISH. (Photo: Oonagh McGibbon)

To Kevin Sparrow for the photography – as always. There is also photography by Andrew Griffin, Oonagh McGibbon, Andrea Hessay and Angela Niemeyer Eastwood (credit given where applicable).

To Olympic judge Peter Holler for taking the time to write the foreword.

We would like to acknowledge and thank the FEI for permission for us to reproduce excerpts and quotations from the FEI Dressage Handbook – Guidelines for Judging and the current FEI Rule Book 2014/15.

We would also like to acknowledge and thank British Dressage for permission for us to extract information and rules from the current British Dressage Rule Book 2015.

Foreword

In 2011 German dressage judge Peter Holler was awarded 5* international O-judge status, making him eligible to judge at the Olympics. 'Of course it is something very special for me,' Peter told Eurodressage; 'I think it shows that people appreciate the expertise and engagement. It is a challenge, but, as dressage is my passion, it is a really great thing.

'I have a very interesting and engaging working life as a PR consultant based in my home town of Koblenz in southern Germany, where we specialize in marketing, human resources and industry, which brings together my journalistic and academic sides. My second life, so to speak, is as an FEI dressage judge, clinician and trainer for which I travel worldwide.

'There are many excellent books on all aspects of dressage. However, there is a continuing need for knowledge and understanding in our modern horse world as the traditional horsemen and women disappear from the stage. This book presents an up-to-date treatise on the theories and practices in modern dressage thinking and training, without losing the perennial basics that have stood the test of time.

'It stands out in its efforts to really explain the why, what and how that are involved in the further education of advanced horses and riders; the sequence photographs in the book bring these aspects to life in a most useful way. It is with great pleasure that I recommend Angela and Andrea's second dressage training book, *Advanced Dressage Training*, to you.'

Peter Holler

Peter Holler, FEI Olympic judge.

Preface

When we embarked on our first book, *Understanding Dressage Training*, we had no idea of the sheer hard work, mental and physical, involved in translating knowledge and experience gained over many years into words and images that would have to stand or fall on their own merit for years to come. This time we did know what to expect and we still did it! Writing turns out to be quite addictive when you are as passionate about a subject as we are – dressage in all its aspects is still something that stirs our respective souls.

In the fifty-plus years in which we have been involved with dressage, the sport has exploded exponentially, and these days FEI-level classes of upwards of thirty are quite normal, while at international level it usually takes two whole days to get through the Grand Prix. Discussions about whether or not the Grand Prix tests should be shortened to take account of media and spectator interest are currently underway. This is unlikely to impact on Rio 2016, and the two sides are implacably opposed at the moment. Only time will tell the outcome and, as ever, there are pros and cons to be considered.

Breeders are producing more and more amazing horses with often breathtaking paces, and the best riders can produce extraordinary results from such mega equine stars. However, in order for less talented riders to cope with such horses there are some rather dubious training methods out there, so our plea is for riders and trainers to keep the welfare and well-being of their horses at the forefront of what they do.

Along the way many people have specialized in dressage, some almost from the cradle, and a whole generation has grown up without the broader knowledge of equestrian sport that used to be the norm. This brings its own challenges, as riders no longer necessarily have personal knowledge of how to produce a competition horse, in peak fitness, and what that involves. The Pony Club, the Riding Club, hunting, eventing and so on, used to provide that information, which now has to be learned from books, magazines or professional yard owners. There is nothing essentially wrong with this, but it can sometimes mean that a deeper relationship with the horse is harder to achieve, and the result can be that signs of potential trouble are not always noticed early enough.

Our book does not cover equine care other than from a training perspective, but there is a wealth of accumulated knowledge out there that would enhance any equine/human partnership – and it is often that depth of knowledge that makes the difference between an average partnership or an amazing one.

Psychology has always been part of any athletic competition, often subliminally, but these days it is acknowledged as being one of the main contributory factors to excellence in any sport – indeed in any of life's ambitions.

They say that you can plan to fail, or fail to plan. Either way, you have talked yourself out of a positive outcome before you start. Technical skills need to go hand in hand with mental commitment, discipline, dedication and resilience.

Mindsets can be changed – what is needed is support, imagination and perseverance.

We have tried to explain the whys and wherefores of dressage training to advanced level as we understand them. Many have done so before us, and many more will do so in the future, but something that could be said more often is that aids are just that: they let the horse know what the rider wants, and when this is understood, the horse should be allowed to do whatever has been asked of him – alone and *unaided* – until something else is required or the horse needs a reminder.

Finally, for your own sanity, that of those around you and that of your horse, remember that the pursuit of *excellence* is what dressage is all about – not perfection! It takes more than one human lifetime to really understand how to train horses and, by the time one might have a few answers, it is time to move on to the next world!

Our hope is that this book contributes another piece to the jigsaw that is equine training.

A and A

Note: We have given horses and humans the designation 'he'; this is for simplicity only and does not signify any slight against the females of either species.

Our riders have been very generous in showing good and less good versions of some movements, to illustrate a point in the text – so please do not be too quick to judge!

Laura Tomlinson, Charlotte Dujardin and Carl Hester on their lap of honour at the London 2012 Olympics.

The FEI

The Fédération Équestre Internationale is the international equestrian governing body, and all official international competitions are subject to FEI rules.

The following is an extract from one of the most often quoted articles from these rules:

Article 401 – Object and General Principles of Dressage

The object of dressage is the development of the horse into a **happy athlete** through harmonious education. As a result, it makes the horse calm, supple, loose and flexible but also confident, attentive and keen, thus achieving perfect understanding with the athlete (the rider).*

These qualities are demonstrated by:

Freedom and regularity of the paces

Harmony, lightness and ease of the movements

Lightness of the forehand and the engagement of the hindquarters, originating from a lively impulsion

Acceptance of the bit with submissiveness/throughness (Durchlaessigkeit) without any tension or resistance

FEI Dressage Rules 2014/15

*Bold type and parenthesis are our additions.

Team GB at WEG 2014. Left to right: Gareth Hughes, Charlotte Dujardin, Michael Eilberg, Carl Hester.

The victors at WEG 2014: Charlotte and Valegro with Alan Davies.

Introduction

The greatest enemy of knowledge is not ignorance, it is the illusion of knowledge.

Stephen Hawking

We hope that you are interested in this book because you have already seen or read our previous one, *Understanding Dressage Training*, or, if not that one, then other books that have helped to take you as a rider/trainer to medium level and now you are aiming for Grand Prix. Whether or not you are interested in competing, perhaps you have some knowledge of what is expected of an advanced horse and rider combination? If so, perhaps we can expand that knowledge even further. If not, we hope that you will find the content of this book educational.

What is dressage?
It is the enhancement of the natural paces via progressive training to produce the maximum brilliance of the paces according to each horse's ability.

What is advanced training?
It is the consolidation of a correct, basic, progressive foundation that allows lateral work, collection, extension and other Grand Prix movements to be taught and demonstrated without tension, stress or resistance. It is the culmination of how each element fits into the overall finished picture.

We make no apologies for the many repetitions in this book as this is how we all learn, and some things just cannot be repeated often enough. We also make much reference to *Understanding Dressage Training* because detailed '*how to*' explanations are within it and it doesn't seem helpful to reproduce them all again. However, since both books cover the same subject, dressage, albeit from a different perspective, and advanced work is only possible with a solid knowledge of the basics, some repetition is inevitable – and, of course, we are bound to recommend that reading both books in tandem would be advantageous!

UNDERSTANDING
Dressage Training

Angela Niemeyer Eastwood
with Andrea Hessay

The front cover of **Understanding Dressage Training** *(published 2011).*

The ideas, exercises and experiences outlined in this book are gleaned from years of reading, observing, riding, training, coaching, judging, watching top trainers at clinics and on video, and attending international competitions and forums, to bring together as much information and knowledge as we could for you to ingest. We give credit wherever possible, and the bibliography references the sources. We have used many photographs to illustrate the text and some of the work shown will be less than perfect, some will intentionally show what should not be done. In most of the photographs it is possible to find some small fault, which is what life is like, and they are the more educational for all that.

What are the requirements for more advanced training?

- A rider with the knowledge, practical experience and ability to train the horse progressively
- A rider with a sufficiently balanced, independent seat
- An able, trainable, willing horse with three correct paces. These days, breeders are more and more conscious of breeding for temperament as well as paces, which is obviously a help in choosing a horse; however, the most naturally talented horse in the world is really only as good as his trainability and rideability. Since horses go how they are ridden, it is the rider who makes the horse, and not the other way round
- A horse with conformation good enough to cope with the demands made on his physique by the more advanced exercises
- An experienced Grand Prix trainer in whom you have trust and confidence to train both horse and rider
- Somewhere suitable to ride – an outdoor manège with a good surface of 20 × 40m as a minimum, and ideally one of 20 × 60m.

Access to an indoor arena is not the luxury it once was, as these days it is possible to hire various arenas around the UK, and in inclement weather, the use of such an arena allows you to plan and to keep to a consistent training schedule

It is, of course, possible to train in a much smaller space but it does limit the likelihood of coping well with overall accuracy, not to mention the extended work and sequence changes. Experience tells us that you really do need to have the use of a correctly measured arena at some point because, if it is too big or too small, it just makes things more difficult than they need to be. For freestyle dressage to music the use of a correctly sized arena is essential so that you can ride your programme in competition arenas with a degree of confidence that it will fit.

ARENA SURFACES

Arena surfaces are crucial. There has been much recent and ongoing scientifically based research into arenas and their maintenance to discover what impact they have on horses and their training. Briefly, the outcome seems to be that many different surfaces are suitable if – and this is a very important 'if' – they are regularly maintained and topped up when necessary. More than one horse has become unlevel or lame as a result of being ridden on an inadequate surface. Ageing and degradation of arena surfaces are other factors to take into consideration, together with overall management of the horses involved. The one thing upon which there seems to be little argument is that soft, deep surfaces where the hooves sink down cause tendon and ligament injuries and should be avoided. Firmer rather than softer surfaces seem to cause less trouble overall.

Obviously, surfaces differ and so riding on a variety of surfaces, including grass, hard surfaces and those with different gradients, can make horses and their balance more adaptable and able to withstand the varying loading patterns which each different surface presents. It can also be that working on only one type of surface makes horses more susceptible to injury through repetitive overloading.

What is suitable for show jumpers, Western horses or driving is not necessarily the optimum for dressage.

(The 2014 FEI's *Equine Surfaces White Paper*, a collection of published scientific papers from the UK, the USA and Sweden, contains considerably more detail for those interested, although it is considered to be a work in progress, and also *Equestrian Surfaces – a Guide.*)

Equine Surfaces White Paper.

EQUINE SURFACES WHITE PAPER 2014

Authors
Sarah Jane Hobbs, Ph.D., University of Central Lancashire, UK
Alison, J. Northrop, M.Sc., Anglia Ruskin University, UK
Christie Mahaffey, Ph.D., Racing Surfaces Testing Laboratory, USA
Jaime H. Martin, Ph.D., Myerscough College, UK
Hilary M. Clayton, BVMS, Ph.D., MRCVS, Michigan State University, USA
Rachel Murray, MA VetMB MS Ph.D., MRCVS, Animal Health Trust, UK
Lars Roepstorff, DVM, Ph.D., Swedish University of Agricultural Sciences, Sweden
Michael 'Mick' Peterson, Ph.D., University of Maine, USA

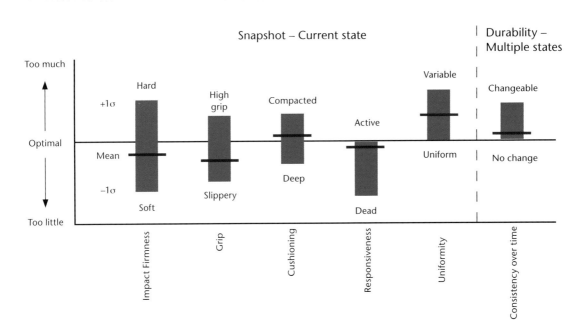

Arena standardization figure.

The arena at Blue Hors Stud, Denmark. (Photo: Angela Eastwood)

The WEG 2014 arena in Normandy, France. (Photo: Angela Eastwood)

TALENT (ABILITY)

Most horses can be trained to medium level, and often to several levels higher – for instance, to Prix St Georges (PSG) and Inter 1 (these two levels constitute the phrase 'small tour'). From then on, however, some innate natural talent for piaffe/passage is desirable to reduce the pressures and stress on both horse and rider. Some horses really are small tour horses, even if they can just about manage passage and/or piaffe, because the level of difficulty can be too much for their natural ability, and thus often for their mental state. There are quite a few horses out there that have burnt out, or become ring shy, or just plain sour due to over-work, incorrect work, or ignorance, and it is only through lengthy and experienced rehabilitation that some of them become rideable again – but seldom at their previous level.

DREAMS AND GOALS

> Every morning you have two choices: continue to sleep with your dreams, or wake up and chase them.
>
> *Unknown*

Dreams are good and necessary. However, realistic, progressive goals work better because they are achievable and reduce the inevitable frustrations along the way – and it is entirely possible that the dreams might end up coming true! Shortcuts are just that, and what has been left out of the training will surface at the higher levels, causing unnecessary problems just when you thought you had it all in hand, so to speak. Using force, or trying to totally dominate your horse, is ultimately doomed to failure as this does not make for a good working relationship, it just produces tension and resistance. You need the horse on your side – so firmness, habit, repetition and clarity, in conjunction with patience, generosity of spirit, a positive attitude, rewards, praise and a sound knowledge of training, are the ingredients for success (whatever that means to you).

FEEL

Feel is one of the most difficult things for a trainer to impart to a rider, but it is possible when the rider learns to tune into the feeling that the horse gives in response to the rider's aids. First, how do the walk, trot and canter affect the rider, and what is the response of the horse to how the rider moves in the saddle? Then comes the feel down the reins – is it light, heavy, equal, resistant, pulling, unyielding, soft, flexible? Feel has a lot to do with personal body awareness, control and balance, together with an open communication system between horse and rider. Feel is, one could say, the coming together of experiences that have been consciously analysed and reproduced, usually in conjunction with a trainer's positive feedback, and translated into something tangible.

Feel should develop over time into something more or less intuitive, and as such, it becomes the essence of dressage – where the horse appears to perform without any noticeable input from the rider. This is when dressage becomes 'art', and a harmonious partnership is a joy to watch.

Dressage has many similarities to ballroom dancing and ballet. When watching good dancing partnerships, everything happens with ease and grace, no one seems to 'do' anything obvious but the steps and the elegance are there for all to see. The two dancers are equal partners, although one is leading and one following, and one or other only takes a more prominent role when,

Riders, the 'crème de la crème' (just a selection): Laura Tomlinson...

briefly, the other one needs support. When everything is in harmony it is not necessary to intervene, as the partners need to learn to cope alone as well as being part of a team. How do they get there? Preparation (no surprise), constant practice (consistency) and control/discipline (benign).

World-class partnerships – for instance Laura Tomlinson, Edward Gal, Hubertus Schmidt, Helen Langehanenberg – all epitomise this: it did not happen by accident or luck, and they repeat their successes on horse after horse.

RIDING

Learning to ride is a conscious acquisition of technique, but riding has to become sub-conscious, your body reacting without apparent conscious thought to what is happening so you 'just do it' – like driving a car, riding a bike, and so on. Sadly, it is as easy to 'just do it' in the wrong way, and that is where correct training comes in.

When the subconscious, automatic state has been reached and you can ride, it is important to ensure that your conscious mind does not become subservient to your subconscious – your body must do what your brain tells it to so that you remain in control of what you do! You need to acquire and maintain mental and physical control in a conscious way.

The devil is in the detail, they say – and it is the detail that will transform your horse and yourself into an advanced combination. The most successful riders never neglect the

Edward Gal...

Hubertus Schmidt...

and Helen Langehanenberg.

smallest detail of training and accuracy – that is how and why they succeed – and then they practise some more!

Nothing is as impressive or as valuable for the training as being able to control the impulsion and the desire to go forward to such an extent that the rider is able to bring his horse to a stand-still from an extended trot or canter without the slightest effort or disturbance. Conversely, departing immediately from the halt into an extended gait is an equal proof of the absolute desire to go forward.

Alois Podhajsky (former Director of the Spanish Riding School in Vienna)

1 The Horse

It is just like man's vanity and impertinence to call an animal dumb, because it is dumb to his dull perceptions.

Mark Twain

Know your horse – his body language, his strengths and weaknesses.

What is his individual way of learning? Is he quick to learn, curious about the world, intelligent, or slow to pick things up and uncurious? Understand what a horse is – approximately 650 kilos of instinct, a prey animal, whose natural reactions to everything and anything are fright, flight, fight, freeze and, in extremis, faint. The horse is a herd animal and he is very open to being led by a leader whom he learns to respect – the hierarchy of a herd is established very early on, seldom with any violence, and with very small, clear gestures.

Fear is a major factor in a horse's make-up – it is how he survives in the wild and **these primitive, involuntary instincts never leave him, regardless of how highly he is trained**. Fear can range from being wary of somewhere or something new, but open to being reassured by his handler/rider that everything is fine, to fleeing first and asking questions later! The real danger is when horse and rider are both in the panic zone at the same time; faced with a charging bull elephant it is sensible to go with the instincts to get away quickly and then regroup. In our rather more sheltered, less wild world the rider needs to be able to manage the situations that occur.

Your horse needs you to be a leader in whom he can trust and have confidence, and ideally, this is established early in his life and/or in his relationship with you. Consistency is the key. If you are consistent, firm and fair, your horse will quickly learn to accept you as his herd leader and give you his respect. However, if you are inconsistent, your horse will become confused and will start to make up his own mind about what he should or should not do. You really do not want 650+ kilos of instinct to find out how big and strong he is and how easy it would be for him to challenge you!

Some horses are spooky, afraid of everything and anything, and lack self-confidence – Anky van Grunsven's famous Grand Prix horse, Olympic Bonfire, was spooky and very unsure of himself and everything around him, and his first outing at PSG was not a success – over time he grew to rely on his rider and trust her implicitly. He became a great competitor in spite of his continued nervousness of the proximity of the crowds. However, it took much patience, skill and experience to get to that point. It is easier all round to try to find a horse with a good, calm temperament who views the world through confident eyes and then all you have to do is keep him like that.

A top international dressage horse is the same species as the hairiest riding school inhabitant – different jobs, different builds, different movement, definitely different amounts of hair, but essentially equine. They like to eat, sleep, wander about, roll, socialize with their companions, eat some more … and they live in the moment. You might agonize for hours about your last ride or an upcoming

Different equines: not Grand Prix Polly...

competition, but be assured that your horse does not.

SUPPORT AND MANAGEMENT

These days our sport has much support outside the rider/trainer duo – owners, sponsors, grooms, physiotherapists, psychologists, nutritionists, sports scientists, sports injury specialists, fitness trainers, vets, dentists, farriers, saddlers and other background supporters. On the basis that prevention is way superior to cure, it is good to develop your own team of advisers – but it is also necessary to have a good knowledge of horse care and stable management yourself. Many competitions have been lost because the horse is not sufficiently healthy, or strong or fit enough to sustain the pressures, and nutrition plays a major part in this – all reputable food manufacturers have qualified and experienced nutritionists who are happy to help horse owners with this aspect of horse welfare. Within reason, it makes good sense to have the horse checked over regularly (perhaps every six weeks or so), but turning yourself and your horse into hypochondriacs in the process is not useful!

QUALITIES

It cannot be said often enough that there is no such thing as a perfect horse or a perfect human. Every one of them and every one of us has got, or will develop, 'issues'. Big horses have their own challenges, small compact horses also have challenges but different ones

from the big horses. Mares and stallions are bundles of hormones, and geldings tend to be much more tractable, although there are always exceptions. Talent and ability are necessary at the top level, but trainability and willingness to work score very highly too. The most talented individual will only get so far on natural ability as there needs to be a willingness to co-operate and to be educated, whilst keeping the spirit intact.

Grand Prix potential is not that easy to spot and is certainly not guaranteed. Some horses get to small tour but show little or no interest

...and Grand Prix WG Rubins Nite.

or talent for piaffe and passage, and thus the careers of these horses are best developed at that level. Others show a natural ability for piaffe and passage, through short steps introduced at a relatively early stage, and/or when they are showing off naturally – these are the horses that, other things being equal, are likely to make it to Grand Prix. However, not all horses have the athletic and mental capabilities of top international horses and, in the end, it is about maximizing the strengths and minimizing the weaknesses of the horse you have in order to produce the best of which he is capable.

Trainability and willingness are more important than ideal conformation, although, of course, the more ideal the 'make' of a potential dressage horse the better.

RIDEABILITY/TRAINABILITY

It is well accepted that dressage horses need to have around 40 per cent natural ability. The other 60 per cent is made up of rideability, trainability, and a willingness to work. Show jumpers need exactly the opposite ratio. Beyond these figures, character, temperament, age and correct training make up the remaining 60 per cent. The degree of rideability does depend, to an extent, on what each rider requires of his horse. Professional riders would have different criteria from amateur riders and would accept a hotter, sharper horse because such qualities are often what make a top horse special. However, what every rider needs is a horse prepared to work with his rider.

It is never a good idea for a horse to find out that he is bigger, stronger and quicker than any human and could pit such assets against that human. Good handling, riding and progressive training should ensure that your horse never finds out just what he could do!

CONFORMATION

So what aspects of conformation do dressage riders consider the most important? Good looks are a matter of opinion, but overall a well proportioned body is likely to be one that looks good and can use itself well. Conformation depends very much on Mother Nature, but maturity definitely comes into the equation so, for instance, a very croup-high young horse might well mature into a horse where the withers are marginally higher than the quarters, which is a good thing. However, being croup high is not desirable in a mature horse as it will be more difficult for such a horse to truly collect. Having said that, however, some horses confound their conformation and produce good quality advanced work.

Other good things are:

*   an elegant fine-featured head, with a kind eye
*   a well set-on neck of proportionate length to the body and which tapers towards the poll, with plenty of space in the throatlash area. (A short thick neck is problematic, as the larger the jowl and salivary gland the more difficult it is for the horse to flex at the poll)
*   well defined withers with the neck coming up and out from them
*   a sloping shoulder together with open elbows, flat knees and sloping pasterns that match the slope of the shoulders
*   when viewed from the front, the legs and feet should be straight
*   when viewed from the front, the chest should not be too wide (the old nagsmen used to say that the optimum width was that of a bowler hat)
*   not too long a back, as this can mean that the horse might struggle with self-carriage in the long term. (Bear in mind, however, that a mare often has a longish back to

Good, not perfect, conformation – there is no such thing as perfect conformation.

accommodate a foal.) A long-backed horse is often more comfortable for the rider
- not too short a back, as this can mean that the horse will tend towards stiffness and will lack optimum suppleness over the back
- strong hindlegs, with a long line from the point of the croup to the hock, shortish cannon bones, with the angles of the joints from croup to pastern in proportion with each other, so that the horse can naturally step under his body and support himself
- when viewed from behind, the lower hindlegs should be plumb-line straight, not turning in or out at the hocks
- four matching, good strong feet to complete the picture; if that isn't the case, then at least the front feet should be a matching pair

Nothing should stand out or draw attention to itself in a well put-together horse. Defects in conformation need to be considered and discussed with a vet before purchase but, if you look around, there are many horses performing well at all levels up to Olympic standard with less than ideal conformation. Good management, a thorough knowledge of equine anatomy and physiology, and appropriate training make up for any less-than-perfect elements of conformation. 'Handsome is as handsome does' is not a bad saying to keep in mind.

For those interested in the detail of particular characteristics of individual horses, *Getting in Touch with Horses* by Linda Tellington-Jones is a fascinating read.

Then there are the paces – and a big impressive trot can blind purchasers to the other less good paces. Ideally you want three correct, forward-going paces (gaits) with

natural rhythm and cadence, and bear in mind that the walk and canter are the two more difficult paces to improve. However, a good four-beat walk suggests that there should be a good canter in there somewhere (and vice versa), whilst the trot is generally considered to be the easiest to adjust and develop. At Grand Prix, the walk is an important constituent part of the test, but it can be that a horse with a huge, expressive overtrack faces disadvantages in learning to shorten the stride for a good piaffe – for example Monica Theodorescu's Whisper – and may develop a lateral or less clear four-beat walk in the process, whereas a horse with a less amazing yet correct walk, such as Carl Hester's Uthopia, would find it much easier to produce a good piaffe.

The paces: walk...

Trot...

Canter.

When thinking of purchasing a horse it is desirable to see him moving loose before riding; this can be an eye opener as to the paces and the type of personality the horse possesses. It also shows whether or not the horse has natural balance and an uphill way of going. As a general rule, we do not buy young, unbroken horses any more as we prefer to feel how the horse is underneath the rider, however green that horse may be. This is very much a personal preference, and of course, unbroken horses are mostly cheaper to buy (and, in this case, it is worth checking out the way in which the youngster has been handled to date). By the by, from long experience we have found that it is good practice to have your new horse's teeth checked very soon after purchase as quite often this has not been done to any standard, or at all, and a pre-purchase veterinary examination is unlikely to highlight any dental problems.

Whilst an extensive knowledge of bloodlines can be valuable, such knowledge comes more into its own when choosing potential Grand Prix horses as foals or youngsters up to three years old, but even then, it is a risky business. If possible, it is better to buy several foals as a bit of a hedge against disappointment, plus there is the huge advantage of those foals living in a herd, preferably with one or more older horses, so that they learn to be respectful and to understand horse hierarchy. Equally, each foal learns a degree of independence as, for instance with three foals, it is less likely that they will bond with each other to the extent that they are distraught when one friend leaves them, for whatever reason. Also, of course, the odds of finding the horse of a lifetime increase the more young horses you have!

Modern breeding methods have produced many quality horses with much better necks and uphill conformation. The neck plays a major role in the concept of putting the horse on the bit, and the better the neck, all other things being equal, the easier it should be to acquire and maintain the advanced outline necessary in a Grand Prix horse. So a horse built on its forehand, or one with an ultra-high head carriage, would not be wise choices. What is needed is a neck neither too low nor too high.

Searching for the ideal Grand Prix horse depends very much on your experience and expertise, your finances, your 'sort' of horse, whether you are looking for a schoolmaster and can accept some limitations of movement and soundness, whether you are looking for an established star, or one whose star is on the rise. (We could add that listening to experienced, objective advice can be really helpful in making your choice.) Whatever your decisions, this can be a wide-ranging and difficult task, and the following are some things to keep in mind:

- Is the horse sensitive?
- Is he hot and sharp, or laid back and calm?
- Does he react willingly and forwards to the aids?
- Does he want to work with you?
- How is his overall temperament?
- How is he in the mouth: is the contact secure and accepting?

- Is he active, elastic, quick in the hindleg?
- Does he show some self-carriage and a natural ability to take weight behind?
- Does he have a good forearm technique?
- What are the pros and cons of his paces?
- Does he, particularly, have a correct walk?
- What is the current level of his piaffe and passage (or half-steps), and are they correct?
- How good is the canter – does it have an uphill tendency?
- What is the significance, for you, of any veterinary or conformation problems that are highlighted in the pre-purchase examination?

Horses with the big, ground-covering walk that is much prized in young horse classes can often exhibit difficulties in collection, as already mentioned. Horses with an excellent piaffe can often be very hot, which, if controlled, is good, but otherwise leads to tension and the use of piaffe as an evasion. Most of the top horses have their strengths and weaknesses, but good training and clever riding can overcome most things if the horse has a good temperament and is willing to work and perform the movements.

How a horse develops is dependent upon his breeding, his family traits, his size and build. Thoroughbreds are bred to develop early and, in general, tend to be on the smaller, lighter side; warmbloods can grow amazingly until they are eight, nine or even ten years old, ending up very tall and built to match. These horses are slow to mature, and are much weaker than they look until fully developed in comparison with other breeds. Smaller and more compact horses mature and become strong earlier than the big, gangly ones who are not sure where their legs are or even how many they have! It is often true that the former are quicker and sharper, at least initially, than the bigger horses, mostly because their balance allows them to be so.

Young, teenage and mature: from novice to International Grand Prix, 2014 Team GB. DV Stenkjers Nadonna, owned by Jane Brewin. Roland Tong...

then Pippa Fisher...

...and Gareth Hughes.

In the end, the choice should be more about your requirements, and the horse's conformation, temperament and suitability, and rather less about bloodlines.

individuality of each horse, and remember that it is up to you to find a way to communicate and co-operate with your particular horse.

CHARACTER, PERSONALITY AND TEMPERAMENT

Talented horses are often among the most intelligent and, by definition, can be more difficult to train because they are sharp, curious, self-opinionated and clever. However, these are traits that are much valued by top riders, and when correctly channelled, these horses will be the ones most likely to show off their expressive paces and fluent way of going.

The horse's character and personality are important factors; never ignore the

Outside the Box

It can be most useful to think 'outside the box' when confronted with, for instance, a highly strung, 'hot' horse who just does not relax, or an anxious, nervous horse who is not responding to normal training methods. Badly fitting tack, conformation and pain issues are also major contributors to what can appear to be an unhappy horse.

Time, patience and experience can be their own reward. However, top trainers such as Kyra Kyrklund and Adelinde Cornelissen, are always open to ideas from other equestrian disciplines to find the key to horses who do not initially respond to more traditional methods of training.

Alternatives available include work in-hand, which has its own chapter and can be truly beneficial when done correctly.

There is also the Tellington TT Touch Equine Awareness Method (just Google it!). Linda Tellington-Jones is a Canadian who has studied, analysed and demonstrated an alternative way of dealing with horses based on many years of observation, trial and error, to produce horses who gain, or regain, their trust and confidence and thus their ability to learn and co-operate.

Animal behaviourists such as Tristan Tucker and Andrew McLean demonstrate the amazing degree to which any horse can be influenced and can learn to accept the most challenging of scenarios because their trust and confidence in the trainer is total. For instance, at the Global Dressage Forum in Holland in 2012, Tristan Tucker rode his own very inexperienced six-year-old mare and worked her under the arch of a huge mechanical back hoe with the engine running (the noise and smoke had to be heard and seen to be believed!). She was totally relaxed and concentrated on her rider. She was also able to cope with Tristan's assistant running behind her and to her side with a whirring chainsaw (do not try this at home!). This must surely be the ultimate test! Thriller, a Grand Prix horse with massive anxiety and relaxation issues at competitions, coped with cameras, shadows, applause, umbrellas, loud noises, being 'chased' by plastic bags and someone bouncing up and down on a large blue ball, whilst being ridden through the Grand Prix. The response training took several months but the result was success in the arena with a totally chilled horse who also coped with the mounted prize giving, something never previously possible.

Tristan uses his response training to enhance the horse's sensitivity and focus on his rider, the outcome of which is that the horse is not dull and unresponsive but quiet and confident. Here it is the concept of learning which is important, not the thing or the event which seems to be a problem. **Whatever happens physically also happens mentally**. Response training is quite a big subject and, as ever, it is important to have sufficient knowledge before using such a method because done incorrectly, counter-productive would be an understatement.

Andrew McLean's method is the result of practical research from 2011 on overshadowing, based on the principle that a horse can only concentrate on one thing that he is learning at a time, by gradual habituation (response prevention) and conditioning the horse to respond, or not to respond, as requested. Since horses learn by repetition, a gradual desensitizing of horses to fear-inducing stimuli works well. Overshadowing has much in common with the idea, first suggested by Pavlov in 1927 and again by Hull in the 1950s, that when an animal is exposed to two different stimuli it will choose one to which to respond, usually the worst or most important. So bolting would be more compelling than responding to your aids, however frantic. Habituating changes the response over time so the bolting instinct is ultimately overtaken, or overshadowed, by the aids – learning to react positively to your aids in whatever environment and under whatever circumstances.

One example of this method was a horse who reacted badly to the noise of the clippers and could only be clipped under sedation (slightly out of context in a book about dressage, although most dressage horses will need to be clipped at some stage). The first step was that the clippers were turned on from a sufficient distance for the horse not to freak out but close enough to be heard. The horse reacted by trying to get away from the noise, so he was immediately sent backwards by a handler for a few steps and then forwards again several times, while the person with the clippers came closer and closer. This stage took a while (this would be individual to each horse and could take several days) until the horse tolerated the noise close by, and in time allowed himself to be touched with the clippers. At every stage the backwards and forwards steps were constantly repeated so that this activity eventually took priority over his fear of the clippers. However, this only works when the horse has his head and neck lowered in a submissive way. With the head up, tense and braced against the movement with the horse using his strength against the handler is not useful – the submissive stance needs to be confirmed first, by repetition, so that it can be combined with the backwards, forwards method.

Again, this is something that requires far more information and practice than we can discuss in depth here – each method has its pros and cons – so it makes sense to investigate and decide which system might work for your horse in your particular circumstances.

BODY LANGUAGE

Always be aware of what the horse is telling you and take note of grinding teeth, tail swishing, ears flat back or ears pricked forwards and close together, as these can be signs that something is amiss – whether discomfort, tension or anxiety.

Grinding teeth can be a sign of stress and anxiety, although if the horse is otherwise relaxed, submissive and working with the rider, it can just be a sign of concentration.

Both ears somewhat back and to the sides, or even just one ear, is usually an indication

Listening ears: 'What do you want? What should we do?'

that the horse is listening to his rider – and listening is just what a rider wants from his horse, so such mobility of the ears is a most desirable trait.

However, very pricked ears, often associated with a high head carriage and tension in the body, suggest that something external has caught the horse's attention, and this could trigger the flight or fight instincts in extreme cases. In other cases, as in our picture, pricked ears just suggest interest.

Ears flat back indicate anger, pain or fear, together with tension and anxiety, so attention to the horse's body language and the surrounding environment should give the clue as to the problem.

Further to the above, horses who suddenly exhibit unusual or out-of-character behaviour, whether merely weird, extreme or violent, do not do so on a whim. There is always a reason and, in our hard-earned experience, it is often associated with discomfort somewhere which, undiagnosed, can develop into pain. Pain can develop into a chronic rather than an acute stage, and then you have a permanently bolshy horse whose only crime is that he cannot tell you in words what the problem is. Horses are seldom naughty: that is a human condition. Always give them the benefit of the doubt and investigate.

Some horses, especially mares, almost constantly swish their tails when ridden, and given that the rest of the horse's body indicates relaxation and focus, this can have more to do with concentration than irritation. Constant tail swishing combined with an open mouth and tension throughout the body obviously suggest a less-than-harmonious partnership. On its own, therefore, a swishing tail doesn't tell you much about how the horse is feeling.

Ears flat back: 'Do not approach or I will be forced to kill you!'

Pricked ears: 'Hello, that looks interesting. What's going on?'

Tail swishing: 'I'm concentrating and this is difficult!'

As an aside, if the horse clamps his tail down permanently or always carries it to one side, there is probably something amiss, perhaps in the back, that should be investigated, as horses generally carry their tails straight and raised when in motion. Familiarity as to how your horse naturally carries his tail would be relevant here.

Horses tend to signal good intentions with soft eyes, flexible lop ears, a soft muzzle and a relaxed body.

Each new horse, whether young or older, novice or advanced, is uncharted territory for even the most experienced rider, and it would be fair to say that this works both ways. A combination takes time to become a partnership, and although this process can take days, it is more likely that it will take weeks and even months. Your horse does not have your intellectual capability and can only learn something that is totally clearly explained to him, with aids that he understands, and with whatever it is that you want him to learn broken down into easy stages.

In some unfortunate cases the partnership never jells, and it is sensible to admit that this

Tail swishing: 'Nope – don't want to, can't make me!'

Relaxing: downtime with my friend – Alan and Valegro, Amsterdam 2015.

can and does happen. Sometimes perseverance is not enough, or is inappropriate, and then a decision needs to be made for the sake of both horse and rider.

SCHOOLMASTERS

Remember that schoolmaster horses will not teach you to become an advanced rider on their own. They have learned to respond to certain aids and stimuli, so it is beholden on the rider to learn what those signals are, and to replicate them sufficiently well for the horse to produce the work he has learned. If you do not ask correctly he will not do it for you; indeed, you might find that you unwittingly initiate various movements that were not intended and everyone ends up frustrated and confused!

Schoolmaster: I don't think so!

Riding an advanced schoolmaster can be a wonderful introduction to the movements and exercises you are aiming for with your own horse. However, in order to remain consistent and able to do their job, schoolmaster horses need 'topping up' quite frequently by an experienced rider, ideally your trainer, whilst you are still learning to ride him. If not, he will soon revert to the easiest course of action for him, which is to misunderstand you, interpret aids as he chooses, and generally do as he pleases!

...Oh, all right then, if I must.

2 Anatomy and Physiology, Muscles and their Development

The will to win means nothing if you do not have the will to prepare.

Juma Ikangaa

This is perhaps as good a place as any to underline that none of the horse's structures was ever intended to be weight-bearing.

These structures are for locomotion only, and, of course, to support and protect the horse's internal organs and to render him as good an athlete as his conformation allows in his natural state.

The fact that the horse has been domesticated, ridden and driven for many centuries in many cultures does not alter the truth of the above statement.

We recommend that you understand the anatomy of the horse, what muscles are involved in the sort of work that is wanted,

how the horse's structures work, and how they can be built up to get them working optimally, so that the work programme and its relevance to your particular horse can be correctly assessed.

There is a mass of accessible literature on this subject, as well as research, which has analysed, via computer techniques, what exactly happens when horses are working. These days horses painted with their musculature on one side and their skeleton on the other are quite prevalent in lecture/ demonstrations around the country, which helps to drive home how the horse moves and what structures and mechanics are involved.

Painted horse, showing the mechanics in action over a jump.

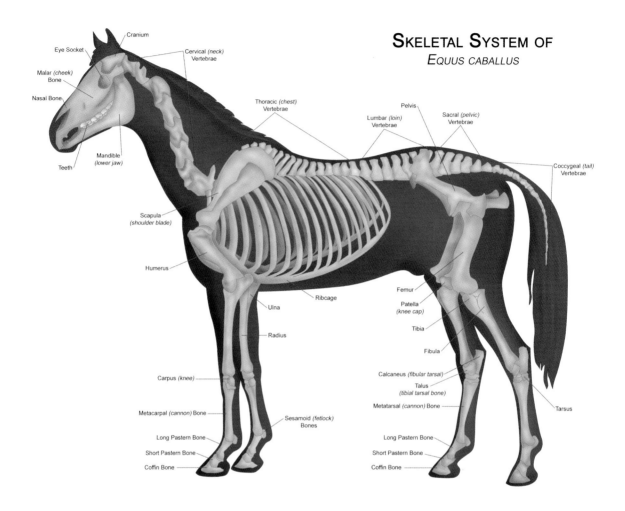

The horse's skeletal structure. (Attribution: WikipedianProlific at the English language Wikipedia [GFDL (www. gnu.org/copyleft/fdl.html) or CC-BY-SA-3.0 (http://creativecommons.org/licenses/by-sa/3.0/)], via Wikimedia Commons)

Volumes have been written about long, deep and round (LDR) – not to be confused with a forceful domination of the front end of the horse by over-strong hand aids (Rollkur). The horse needs to relax over his back, seeking the bit forwards and downwards, keeping the withers up and, ideally, with his nose slightly in front of the vertical. We covered this in Chapter 7 of *Understanding Dressage Training*, but in this book we want to go deeper and examine the process from a more informed viewpoint so that the processes of what has to happen in the horse's body are clarified.

There are two anatomical structures, or systems, which allow us to produce a horse that is working 'on the bit' and 'through from behind'. Dr Gerd Heuschmann calls them 'the upper contraction system' (the ligament system of the cervical spine and back from the poll via the withers to the sacrum) and the 'lower construction system' (the trunk, abdomen, pelvic area and hindquarters). These are easy

Rollkur: a forced, deep position and bend, on the hand.

Long, deep and round: relaxed, unforced stretching.

enough terms to understand even though the physiology behind them is more complex. The two systems are inter-dependent, and the horse only functions effectively and athletically when they are correctly deployed.

A useful exercise, and one that most therapists are likely to use to test the horse's reflexes when undertaking an examination and before commencing any treatment, is the manual manipulation of the horse's back and spine. With care, this is something that can be done by the layman. The specific touching of prescribed areas stimulates a reaction to check that muscles are functioning correctly – or not. There are several stimuli points on the back, at the ribcage, on the back behind the saddle and on the quarters. Some experience is necessary and care needs to be taken that the horse does not over-react and kick out or

move suddenly. The reactions or otherwise give considerable information about what muscle groups might be in spasm and require remedial work. The pictures can only give a clue as to how the above is done, so it is important to work with a therapist to ensure that you do this correctly.

The ability to ride the horse forwards and downwards is a fundamental requirement for any stage of training, from novice to Grand Prix. It is a position that enables the horse to carry the rider without undue effort – but it is also a position that makes the horse vulnerable, as his flight/fright instincts are surrendered to the rider. Hot, anxious horses are understandably reluctant to do this, so it follows that the practical application is much enhanced when the theory is understood.

Manipulation: working on the back and hindleg stimuli points.

Just being horses: relaxing out at grass at Carl's. (Photo: Andrea Hessay)

Horses can graze for hours on end with their necks stretched out and down without stiffening or muscle fatigue. However, they keep on moving around and alter the position of their necks in so doing.

When we ride, the horse's musculature has to cope with the weight of his own head and neck and also with our weight. This changes the dynamics, and means that all positions of the horse's head and neck need to be altered regularly to avoid fatigue and stress in the horse's body. Bear in mind that 60 per cent of the horse's weight is carried over the front legs – that is, one third of the horse's total bodyweight, the head, neck and shoulders contributing most of it, and that is before having to cope with our extra weight.

What follows here is a simplistic, albeit lengthy, version of the complex processes that allow horses to move when ridden – be aware that much more rigorous, scientific and anatomical explanations exist and are easily accessed for those who prefer more in-depth, detailed information.

There are four abdominal muscles that work in concert, like a corset or a hammock, to keep the internal organs protected and able to function. The rider's leg aids are instrumental in starting the process of *throughness* via light touches/nudges at the point where the girth sits. Through contraction of the muscles of the chest (sternum) together with the lower muscles of the pelvic area, the horse's body closes up. Consequently, the pressure in the lower abdomen area rises and the internal organs are lifted, they support the spine and, in that process, the *transverse processes* (the bony attachment sites from the vertebrae to the spinous muscles) open and create more space between them and the ribs. The mobility of the spine increases, thus allowing the back to swing more easily and increasing lateral mobility at the same time. The pelvis tips up, the loin area lifts and pulls the main back muscle, the *longissimus dorsi*, taut, which in turn lifts the whole of the back to the fourteenth rib and exposes the lowest part of the back, where the saddle should sit, just behind the withers. Tension in the hindquarters is released, and the hindlegs can step freely forward underneath the belly of the horse because the contraction of the abdominal muscles has lifted the ribcage and organs out of the way. This process also achieves a lift in the withers, the transverse processes come upright, and the *nuchal* ligament (the ligament that follows the upper line of the neck to the withers and connects with the supraspinous ligament towards the tail) softens so that the head and neck can lower.

If the horse is not ridden from behind to the contact, as above, the back cannot lift, the pelvis is in the wrong position, as is the spine which is pushed down. The transverse processes close, with the result that there is less room between each vertebra, the spine tightens, the withers drop and the neck cannot lower correctly. (This is easily spotted by a 'broken' neck and/or a solid underneath neck muscle, both of which are the result of the horse being pulled into a shape by the rider's hands.) There is no swing in the back, and the gluteal muscles in the hindquarters are under too much tension to allow the hindlegs to come underneath the horse's belly.

Instead of achieving a free-moving horse that is flexible from head to tail, the opposite is the result.

Musculature

Muscles are fibrous bundles of cells which contract and expand (or relax). There are fast-twitch muscles (white fibres) for power and

fast contractions, and slow-twitch muscles (red fibres) which contract more slowly and provide the endurance capacity. Many muscles are dormant much of the time, and their activation is triggered by work (hence the need for a warm-up before a work session). They require oxygenation from the blood vessels surrounding them, and there are two sorts of oxygen metabolism: aerobic, which is with oxygen; and anaerobic, which is without oxygen (lactic acid).

Lactic acid build-up is necessary for muscle development, but the work that triggers this ***must*** be short-lived, followed by a period of relaxation in order for the oxygen to restore the aerobic balance so that the horse does not seize up.

Genetically, horses vary in their share of the two muscle types. Some horses have more capacity for endurance, and some are more inclined towards fast work with a quicker, higher fatigue rate. However, training can mitigate the differences to a certain extent to compensate for the particular horse's predisposition.

Muscles are able to contract in three ways:

- concentrically – the muscles shorten when contracting (for example, when you lift a weight with one arm, the elbow angle is more acute and the biceps come into play)
- isometrically – the muscles neither shorten nor lengthen (as when you hold the weight with an outstretched arm)
- eccentrically – the muscles lengthen in the contraction (hold the weight but do not fully extend the arm)

So, for the horse:

- concentric = acceleration
- isometric = contraction within a specific posture
- eccentric = deceleration and collection

However, concentric contraction (acceleration) is required to get into eccentric (collection) mode.

Endurance development comes with basic circles, lateral work and stretching, in all three paces. Power development includes extension and collection, transitions to, from and within the paces, together with relaxation breaks. All these elements are part and parcel of advanced work.

The more advanced the work, with an uphill frame and collection, the more it will be biased towards eccentric contraction. That is why some concentric work needs to be included, without keeping the horse in isometric work for long periods – so never forget regular stretching and relaxation.

The big responsibility for the rider is to know how much is enough. Fatigued muscles cannot function correctly, so neither can the tendons and ligaments attached to them, and that is when trauma occurs. Dressage horses are very prone to suspensory ligament problems as there is no muscle attached to these ligaments to limit overstretch. Tendons and ligaments have no nerves or blood vessels and have to cope with enormous strains and stresses when the horse is moving; injuries to these take considerable time to heal, and there is little that the veterinary profession can do to alleviate or hasten the process, despite the claims made of the various creams, potions and injections available to those owners who like spending money!

A good rule of thumb is to repeat an exercise only two or three times then, improvement or not, do something else, and go back and try again after a break. Such a regime lessens the impact on tendons and ligaments and helps to keep them under the tension they need to keep working correctly without undue strain. Increasing core strength and body suppleness reduces the risks of mechanical breakdown. Horses are fragile, sensitive creatures and it is vital to minimize stress and strain as far

as possible. It is good to vary the work so that repetitive injuries are sidetracked by progressive and intelligent use of training exercises.

This is, essentially, interval training, with close attention to the Scales of Training. Interval training was once very much in fashion for event horses, and it is back, as it helps cardiovascular development and limits stress to short bursts, with recovery times in between, challenging and strengthening the musculature without over-tiring the horse.

Multi-discipline training is as good for horses as it is for humans, and this can include:

- canter work on a track (such as round a field or on a training gallop)
- hacking out (with purpose!)
- lungeing
- pole and cavalletti work
- time on the horse walker
- treadmills
- jumping
- working on different surfaces, such as on the beach, up and down hills
- swimming

These days there is a trend towards turning out even Olympic-level horses daily, and in some cases they live out and work from grass. This has been found to be the key to keeping particularly highly strung horses calm and relaxed.

In all the talk of training, obedience, submission and so on, it is as well to remember that a horse is a horse and not some mechanized vehicle for our ambitions – let him go out, roll in the mud, eat grass, relax and be – a horse.

A resting horse has a heartbeat of around thirty beats per minute (b/m). During a Grand Prix test, research has shown that the rate seldom exceeds 150b/m. Thus the cardiovascular system (the method by which oxygen is delivered to the blood vessels and muscles around the heart) has to work five times as fast as from the resting state, though this is still quite a bit less than for other sport horses – for instance, competing polo ponies and cross-country horses typically have rates between 170 and 240b/m.

With dressage horses it is much more about building stamina and strength than a requirement for fast bursts of speed. Too much low-level work will not do the job,

while too much high intensity work can cause damage: balance is the key. If you go through a session of, say, forty-five minutes, at the end of which no one is sweating, then the chances are that you have not actually worked the horse and thus muscle development and increased strength are unlikely to have occurred.

The skill is to produce a fit, sound horse, strong enough to do the job, with minimum wear and tear!

Fit and strong: well muscled, in beautiful condition.

3 The Rider

The horse shall be favoured above all other creatures for to thee shall accrue the love of the master of the earth.

Extract from the Koran

The rider: what to aim for!

Know yourself and your body. Acknowledge your physical and mental limitations without allowing yourself to make them excuses for not being the best you can be.

- What physical limitations do you have – is there anything you can do about them?
- Are you fit, or, at least, fit enough?
- What shape and size are you – how does this impact on your riding and on your choice of horse?
- What is your temperament? How do you react to challenges or problems?
- Are you patient or impatient, calm or prone to stress?
- Are you intellectual or instinctive (bearing in mind that you can be both)?

- Are you brave or fearful – generally – when something new comes up?
- Do you worry about making a fool of yourself?
- Are you a natural communicator or someone who keeps everything inside – an extrovert or an introvert?
- Are you conscious of your own and other people's body language?
- Are you aware of your strengths and weaknesses?
- Are you aware that, just by being human, you are a natural predator?
- Are you a fighter or a victim?
- How do you learn?
- What type of learner are you?
- How are your levels of focus and concentration?
- Do you prefer to have a go and find out, by trial and error, how to do something?
- Do you like to be shown visually?
- Do you prefer to have everything explained to you before trying something new?
- Do you need to write everything down, learn it, and then try?
- Do you question what you are told, or just blindly follow instructions, without understanding fully what you are doing?

Training any animal is all about patience, repetition, and taking the time to make a habit. It is essential to use a system of praise and reward that demonstrates clearly that the correct response is the one required.

If you want your horse to learn to halt, it is not useful to pat him if he moves off without your consent. The reward needs to come when he stands in response to a command (aid), so that the association is made between the command and his response. Missing this moment by even a few seconds can establish just the sort of behaviour you do not want – the speed of correction is paramount. This is a variation on clicker training, often used to train dogs, and equally effective with horses – done correctly.

Horses use a variety of signals to indicate that we should follow their behaviour and reduce our levels of stress or aggression. This applies whether they are ridden or handled from the ground, inside the stable or outside. If we mistake these clues for disobedience, indifference or distraction, we are unwittingly starting conflict. Sometimes this is inevitable, but generally, a change of approach from the human can trigger a similar response in the horse.

Think about it – if someone is shouting or being aggressive, do you initially turn away? Do you dislike such unpleasant and often loud behaviour, and do you try to avoid such confrontations by being reasonable and calm? When you communicate with your horse, do you shout first? Sometimes whispering is all that is needed.

Good training of the horse results from correct riding and training of the rider, and not the other way round.

Top riders can achieve amazing results with what seem to be 'ordinary' horses. In general, a mediocre rider will only get so far with a talented horse. Also, a mediocre horse will not do much to change you as a rider, but a good horse could help make you a better rider.

Applying theory and common sense goes a long way to preparing a rider for advanced work. In all cases, if the basic Scales of Training have been followed and the horse is correctly muscled and supple, then the more advanced

exercises are not particularly difficult for him. Problems arise if the basic work is lacking.

Psychologists talk about the stages of learning, broken down into four sections:

- *Unconscious incompetence* – you do not know that you cannot ride (ignorance is bliss!)
- *Conscious incompetence* – you have some experiences which make you acknowledge that you really do not know how to ride
- *Conscious competence* – you can ride reasonably well but only if you consciously think about what you are doing and focus on your riding: you are not on 'automatic pilot'
- *Unconscious competence* – your riding is automatic, you know what to do, when and how; you can concentrate on your horse and the environment in which you find yourselves

In fact, with a little imagination, these are stages that you could also relate to your horse as he goes through his training!

As a rider, but particularly as an advanced rider, you need to develop the ability to focus and concentrate on what is happening right now – the past is gone, the future has not happened, so the 'here and now' must be your task. For instance, there is no such thing as very straight – your centre line, your halt, your changes are either straight or they are not; there is no middle ground. Likewise, concentration is either on or off. So initially, concentration has to be learned, like any other skill.

Psychologists also talk about 'circles of concentration'. They draw six circles, spanning out from a very small circle in the middle through six stages to the largest outer circle:

- The sixth circle, the largest one, is akin to *'Who am I, what am I doing here, I want to go home, I hate dressage'*

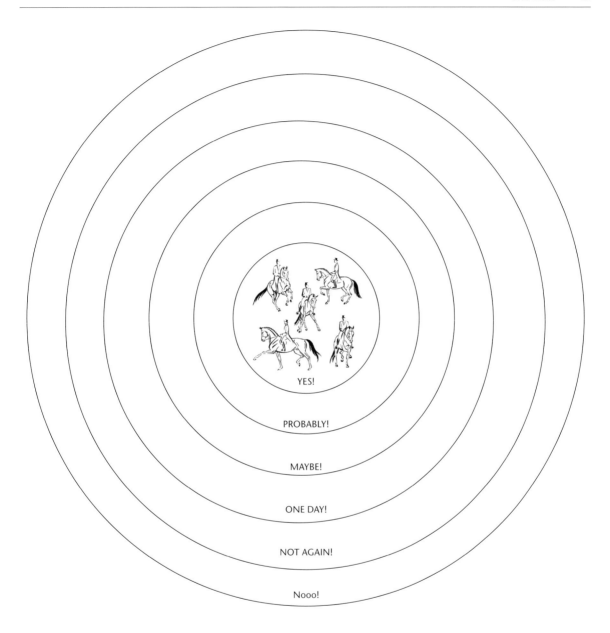

YES!

PROBABLY!

MAYBE!

ONE DAY!

NOT AGAIN!

Nooo!

Circles of concentration.

- The fifth circle is 'OK, *we are here, but too easily put off by outside influences such as "I must win today otherwise ...", my horse does not like plants, arena markers, other horses, people with umbrellas, etc.'*
- The fourth circle gives you improved focus, but you can still be upset by, for instance, a mistake in a movement, going wrong in the test, and so on
- The third circle is still giving you problems: for instance, you tense up as you go down the centre line and your horse responds – or he tenses up and backs off and you respond by becoming tense yourself

- The second circle is where you are both doing very well, the movements are coming up smoothly, then something happens and you lose it for a moment, although you can regain the focus quite quickly now
- The first, and smallest circle, is where you are both totally focused, nothing from outside can get to you, and the fluency of the movements and the way of going is as perfect as is possible

This last one is, of course, the circle of concentration towards which you need to aim, but it does not happen in five minutes – a lot of experiences come in first, both positive and less so. All your experiences add up to self-confidence and self-belief so that the training pays off and the first circle is within range. (NB: a mark of ten is excellent, not perfect.)

Various strategies are available to every rider to help with their mental development, and can include relaxation techniques, 'belly breathing', positive visual imagery, key words and actions, positive self-talk, and identifying both 'what if' and 'worst case' scenarios. Sports psychology boasts a very extensive library of books and videos, and an increasing number of professionals, and is well proven across all sports to help athletes improve their abilities in every sphere of their sport.

Then there are the muscles – your own and those of your horse – and their development through training. Get your *own* muscle development and fitness wrong, or don't bother with it, and you will really struggle to ride competently at the top level (actually any level) without over-straining your muscles – including your heart, which is a muscle. You will be out of breath, you will rapidly lose strength, focus, and the ability to concentrate, then you will not be able to sit to your horse's movement or control it, and your balance will be adversely affected.

With the horse it is again your responsibility. Fatigue and over-straining will be no different for him if he is not prepared and worked in a progressive way that ensures his fitness and health.

There is a close correlation between an unfit, over-worked horse and the vet!

Very seldom does a horse wilfully misunderstand, and the rider/trainer should always question *himself* if the horse does not do what is expected. Always keep to the forefront of your mind that his 'mistakes' are, almost without exception, *your* mistakes (or those of someone who rode or trained the horse before you), which you need to correct.

There are far more problem riders than there are problem horses.

4 The Independent Seat, Posture

In riding a horse we borrow freedom.

Helen Thomson

Horses go how you ride them, and how you ride them totally depends on your posture, body awareness and balance.

This is the crux of the whole thing: if you do not have a totally independent, balanced seat, and are not sitting centrally in the saddle at all times, your horse will be limited by your limitations.

...and Ulla Salzgeber (former German Olympians) – yes, the poll is too low

Being bipeds (two-legged) – that is, vertical – we use our bodyweight and tend to lean forwards rather than backwards while we engage with whatever we are doing with our hands. So we are pre-programmed to use our hands first and above all else when we ride, together with a forward inclination of our upper body. We also tend to concentrate on what is happening in front of us, which is not a good thing all the time, as the horse's engine is behind us. We look down, which rounds the shoulders and collapses the posture and so, crucially, we are not looking where we are going – which our horses definitely are!

Good positions, not far off perfect! Heike Kemmer...

Humans are hand fixated – we do most things with one and/or two hands – and we also concentrate on what is in front of us.

Not so good: rider looking down with some loss of posture... (Photo: Angela Eastwood)

Leaning forwards... (Photo: Oonagh McGibbon)

On the ground, humans balance by keeping everything in line from the top of the head to the heels – any deviation from this position compromises our balance. Therefore in theory, sitting on a horse should be a bit like standing, with slightly bent knees. This should not be challenging as we need this vertical position to follow the movement of the horse whilst maintaining our own balance.

The *'chair seat'*, where the rider's upper body is behind the leg position, means that the rider is always *'behind the movement'* of the horse and plays continual catch-up in terms of forward momentum. Conversely, a hovering seat with a permanent forward inclination of the upper body, balancing on the stirrups and gripping up, means that the rider is always *'in front of the movement'*: like this his influence is much reduced, and any deviant movement of the horse is likely to unbalance or even unseat the rider.

Leaning back, heel up. (Photo: Angela Eastwood)

The optimum position should free the rider to look around without losing balance. Think of sitting quietly rather than sitting still: the latter suggests no movement, when in fact it is vital to have sufficient flexibility to cope with the moving horse.

The optimum position: Charlotte on Valegro.

It is relevant for riders to ponder the difference between gaining an independent seat and the act of sitting.

Realistically, only a rider who can absorb the horse's movement is likely to be able to improve – that is, train – the horse. Thus it takes many years to truly develop what an observer would declare to be easy and unobtrusive. Riding is a sport that makes high physical demands of the rider and, in common with all sports, the rider is totally responsible for his own fitness and competence. In the early stages it is probably best to seek help in acquiring the requisite independent seat.

The horse moves in a wave from back to front and also laterally from side to side, so the rider needs to sit well enough on both seat bones, and with sufficient suppleness, to follow the movement so as not to disturb the horse's rhythm. This requires core stability to maintain balance whilst keeping the seat quiet and the legs loose from the hips, so that the joints can act as stabilizers and shock absorbers. A constantly nodding head

suggests that the rider is not sitting as just described.

In the walk, a good position will enable the rider to extend the arms forwards, keeping a slight bend at the elbows, in order to follow the natural movement of the horse's back and the necessary nodding of his neck and head. This allows the horse to lower his neck, release the underneath muscles, free the shoulders and step out actively. Stiff, set arms and hands constrain the horse's head and neck movement, stifle the walk and cause the rhythm to become slow and often irregular.

In the trot and canter, the rider needs to follow the movement of the horse using the core muscles to maintain the necessary balance which, in turn, allows the rider to influence the pace by moving more, or less, according to what is required.

The rider's shallow breathing and a collapse in the sternum will interrupt the flow from the rider to the horse, blocking the movement and restricting the forwardness of the pace. In addition, if the rider clamps his thighs and knees, the horse will not easily drop his head and neck as the wave from behind is broken and, again, the forwardness is lost.

On the other hand, regular deep breathing, together with an upright position and just enough tension in the core muscles to sustain the position, allows the rider to find a deeper, more central and relaxed position in the saddle, sitting equally on both seat bones. In this way, the rhythm and tempo of the paces are more easily influenced by the rider as the horse feels free to move forwards. Transitions can then be ridden by the use of the seat (weight aid), a light restraining rein aid followed by a slight softening of the finger pressure on the reins, so that the contact remains elastic, thus keeping the fluency and maintaining the rider/horse unit.

More good positions to aim for: Charlie Hutton…

Andreas Helgestrand…

…and Adelinde Cornelissen.

Essentially, your body is your communication tool.

CONTACT/CONNECTION

'On the bit' means contact. This suggests that the horse is flexed at the poll (which is actually a slight rotation of the first cerebral vertebra), soft in the jaw and quiet in the mouth. However, this is not the whole picture. 'Contact' not only refers to the bit, the reins and the hands, but also to the rider's posture and balance which, in turn, allow the horse to work from behind over a relaxed back to the contact.

However, we should talk first of all about suppleness, as it comes before contact in the Scales of Training and is one of the most important aspects, of the many important aspects, in the progressive training of any horse.

What is suppleness? There are two instances – longitudinal and lateral. Where things go wrong is that people become over-obsessed with lateral suppleness when actually, **it is longitudinal suppleness that is crucial and needs to come first**.

So what specifically is longitudinal suppleness? It is when the horse relaxes and stretches over his topline from back to front: that is, from the activity of the hindlegs, over the back through the poll into an elastic, submissive contact, to establish the self-carriage relevant to the level of training. As the horse progresses up the levels, this becomes even more essential as he must have the full use of his back, and thus the power and energy of the hindlegs, without tension or stiffness anywhere in his body.

Lateral suppleness refers to a flexibility at the poll which allows sideways suppleness, equally to left and right, through the body for the correct riding of corners, circles, all lateral work, flying changes, pirouettes – in fact wherever flexion (that is, positioning) is part of the required work. Excessive flexing from side to side, without correct longitudinal suppleness, does nothing to establish lateral flexion and is more about a lack of stability at the base of the neck than correct flexion of the poll.

The combination of both longitudinal and lateral suppleness is necessary for a horse to achieve self-carriage and to work in a relaxed and balanced manner from behind to the contact (connection), i.e. on the bit.

On the bit and through: Michael Eilberg on the Half Moon Stud's Half Moon Delphi, Team GB at WEG 2014.

So, as you can see, contact is really too simplistic a term for what is actually required for a true connection. The aids – the seat, leg and hand – start the process:

80 per cent seat, 15 per cent leg and 5 per cent hand.

The rider's seat and legs encourage the horse to step under himself, allowing the joints of the hindlegs to flex. This releases the energy forwards and upwards through the flexed and lifted back, to the arched neck, the poll and into the jaw, where it meets the rein contact and then, cyclically, back to the hindlegs via the abdominal muscles, which lift the back. This allows the whole process to be repeated.

The clue to riding a horse from back to front – that is, from the engine forwards – is never to think of pulling back or taking back the reins, but rather to think of the horse working forwards into the contact, reaching it and reacting to the aids in a soft, submissive fashion.

When the horse is connected, supple and 'on the bit', half-halts can come 'through' and balance the horse.

Hopefully, the above rather long-winded explanation underlines why it is so important to develop an independent seat. If we cannot maintain our own balance, we stand little chance of helping the horse with his balance, which we compromised by sitting on top of him in the first place.

The horse's movement constantly displaces the rider, who has to learn to follow the movement to stay on and then influence the horse with the seat.

It also underlines the importance of the practical application of all the Scales of Training, as the ultimate aim is to reproduce perfect balance and harmony, enabling the horse to attain the highest degree of collection.

RIDER FITNESS

Most top riders are very aware of their own fitness, and the necessity to be as athletic as they expect their horses to be. Almost all do other exercising beyond riding, however many horses they ride in a day, and focus on their own bodies to the extent that they have excellent core stability, suppleness, stamina, strength and balance.

Top riders such as Dutch Olympian Adelinde Cornelissen have taken fitness to encompass physical and mental strength, to ensure that they get the best out of themselves and their horses. Adelinde has a complete fitness programme that also takes account of how she copes mentally with the physical demands of that programme. She uses exercises from other disciplines such as ballet, boxing, kick boxing, running, trampoline work, beam work, running techniques and so on, to cross-train. Her personal trainer, Tjalling van den Berg, says 'You only train yourself when you come out of your comfort zone', and her mental coach, John van Apeldoorn, agrees. Adelinde views the two aspects as a balance – mental fitness aids physical fitness, and vice versa – and in parallel with what she expects from her horse. She also feels that it is the rider's duty to be sufficiently fit and balanced to aid their horse through his training.

However, you can become so fit and strong that you ride with strength rather than feel, so be aware of this as you train.

Posture

Posture on and off the horse is not different to

Balinese women carrying loads on their heads, demonstrating an everyday balanced, upright posture.

any great degree, as good posture is a habit. Think of the many women worldwide who think nothing of balancing large containers on their heads while walking miles over uneven ground.

Achieving this desirable state is less about having the perfect physique than about knowing your own body, how your posture is on the ground, and making the most of what you have. Everyday activities set up secondary postures which, over time by their repeated patterns, cause us to lose the flexibility and suppleness with which most of us were born. Young babies of eight or nine months can sit at a perfect 90-degree angle, something which tends to elude most adults!

An example to live up to: Sophie Wells, Grade IV Para Olympian, at the Global Dressage Forum 2014 on Katholt's Bossco, a seven-year-old gelding by Blue Hors Don Schufro.

Ideal posture combines minimal muscle work with minimal joint loading, and correct balance depends on each part of the body being in a position relative to each other part. Most people spend more time each day in less-than-perfect posture off the horse than they do on it, and this is a major problem. How are you sitting now while you read this?

Sitting upright, controlled and balanced, the rider can engage the core muscles and use the pelvis, releasing power and energy. Sitting hunched up, stiff, and/or round shouldered, gripping with the thighs and knees, all result in the difficulty of remaining balanced. The rider is weak and exhausted just from the effort of staying on.

All the much repeated positional messages from trainers to riders will be of no avail if the rider is simply bringing a totally incorrect posture to his or her riding.

Stretching

What do most animals do when they wake up or move after a period of rest? They move around and stretch.

LEFT: Pilates: cat stretching.

BELOW: Yoga: horse stretching.

Pilates is a really good form of exercise as it is unaggressive, and you can do as much or as little as your body will allow, and there is always a warm-up phase at the beginning of a Pilates session. Most riders would benefit from a short Pilates-based series of exercises on the ground before starting to ride.

If this were to be combined with being lunged regularly – once a week, and preferably more often – riders with an independent seat would be the norm rather than the rarity they are! Staying on a horse requires balance and body control, and no amount of gripping will do it. Trying to sit still is not very useful as the horse moves you, and you need to learn to move with the horse. Learning to sit quietly and in balance requires core strength, which is something that can be developed. Some professional riders (Ulla Salzgeber, for example) have regular lunge sessions to improve their seat, and also work with computer-generated systems for similar reasons. Other riders put themselves through stirrupless sessions to improve their balance and feel. Riders at the Spanish Riding School in Vienna are lunged on a daily basis for a minimum of six months before they are allowed to progress to having reins and they are all, without exception, experienced, talented riders when they get there!

Developing an independent seat: on the lunge at the Spanish Riding School.

THE SUM OF ALL THE PARTS

The independent seat involves the whole body – head and neck, shoulders, forearms, elbows and hands, core abdominal muscles in conjunction with back muscles, seat bones, hips, thighs, knees, calves, ankles and feet. If the rider is in balance, can sit centrally and independently, the body can be controlled. Riders with a long torso need to take care to strengthen their upper body via exercises to compensate for what can be a weaker musculature.

The position of the forearm muscles affects the quality of the contact through the reins, so the arms should be carried with level shoulders, bent soft elbows, supple flexible wrists, and the hands with thumbs uppermost (that is, not with the back of the hands flat) and on top, all fingers closed round the reins, especially the ring and little fingers, but not with a tight and rigid fist. The wrists should be carried vertically, otherwise rein aids are given with the arms and shoulders, which leads to pulling. When the reins are held correctly the contact is even and secure for the horse. The thumbs should form a 'tent' or 'roof' on top of the index fingers so that there is no tension within the hand and the shock-absorbing actions of the shoulders, elbows, wrists and hands are not impaired. One physical disadvantage that some riders have is arms that are too short, which impacts on the ideal position mentioned above, so some compromise is necessary. This usually takes the form of slightly longer reins, carried a little higher.

The rider's legs should hang comfortably against the horse's sides with the stirrup on the ball of the foot with knees and ankles soft enough to act as shock absorbers, while being free to create small, controlled aids.

The leg position, taken as part of the overall balanced posture, is really crucial. The thighs should be long, with loose, slightly bent knees, not in any way clamped on to the saddle, the calves stretching down without tightness or tension, and the aids effectively given with the calf or the inside of the ankle: not the heel, not a turned-out foot, and only using the spur when needed. The lower calf should remain softly against the horse's ribcage so as to maintain a soft connection as the horse moves. Riders with short legs need to spend more time stretching their muscles to allow their legs to lengthen as far as possible.

So, for the aids to work through to the horse, the rider's upper body needs to be:

- erect
- eyes forward
- head and neck straight
- shoulders dropped
- elbows bent
- core muscles engaged without tension
- seat bones taking equal weight
- hips open and relaxed
- legs long (as above)
- feet resting on the stirrups

The legs need to be easily moved into whatever position they need to be so they are most effective and, in general, would lie on the girth, moving with the horse. If, on the other hand, the rider clamps the knees and thighs on to the saddle, the supple forward movement of the horse is hindered, the horse will hold his back stiff and tight against the clamping he feels and, in addition, the rider is unable to sit correctly, comfortably and independently.

Dancers usually have beautifully balanced posture, as do skaters – if you have some free time, take up ballet, tap, ballroom, salsa, zumba, line dancing, ice skating … if not, try walking! This is something most of us do anyway, just to get about, and there is

Good example of an independent seat: Isabell Werth (German Olympian) on Satchmo.

Ballerina, with a poised and balanced posture.

a technique to walking to improve balance and posture (*see* Chapter 4 in *Understanding Dressage Training*).

If you do no more than just change the way you walk it is hard to ignore the benefits. Relate this new way of walking to what you require from your horse: being upright, in balance, supple, using the joints, taking level steps, with the weight evenly distributed over both feet. The desired outcome is the ability to move freely forwards with energy, ease and the efficient use of the heart, lungs and musculature.

Introduce this new way of walking as you would introduce something new to your horse: gradually and progressively. Done properly, or even partially, it should transform the way you look, how you feel and how you ride. Not everyone will be able to do all of it, but think about the benefits that it will bring:

- recruitment of correct muscle groups
- alignment of body and a more elegant aspect
- increased oxygen and energy levels
- some relief from aches and pains

- looking where you're going
- positive and empowering self-confidence

It has to be worth a try, and all from doing something you are doing anyway.

Adelinde comments:

The main thing we want is to turn our horses into athletes, so ask yourself 'What do I need to do for that?' It is the rider who has to change their attitude and find the way.

Change the way you walk and reap the benefits: in this photo, how lots of us walk; in the next...

...how we should walk.

5 Saddles, Stirrups, Shoeing

If the world was a truly rational place, men would ride side saddle!

Rita Mae Brown

Putting a saddle on the horse's back immediately restricts his movement. Sitting on top of the saddle on the horse's back can only make things worse!

So it is really important that the saddle fits the horse, and the rider, so well that such problems are minimized. Undue pressures on the back, the withers and the shoulders need to be addressed and eliminated so that the horse can move with maximum freedom and no discomfort.

Horses are asymmetric, so a saddle fitter needs to assess how the saddle can assist in rectifying any problems of conformation. Training issues, such as crookedness, are just that, and the best saddle and saddle fitter in the world will not be able to solve such problems.

As horses mature their body structure changes, withers become more pronounced, shoulders develop and muscles attain better definition. Regular checking to ensure that the saddle is still doing the best job possible is essential.

Master Saddler Mark Fisher uses the Pliance testing system, which measures exactly how saddles distribute pressure across the horse's back. These pressures come first of all from the horse's individual conformation – whether he is wide, narrow, high or low withered, upright in the shoulder, has a dipped back, whether the forelegs are free at the elbow or tied in, and so on. Then comes the rider's size, shape and weight, and the work that

the horse is required to do, and, finally, the saddle itself. The more advanced the level at which the horse works, the more pressures can occur. Extreme designs, with very deep, curved seats that enhance the rider's comfort, are not always compatible with the shape of

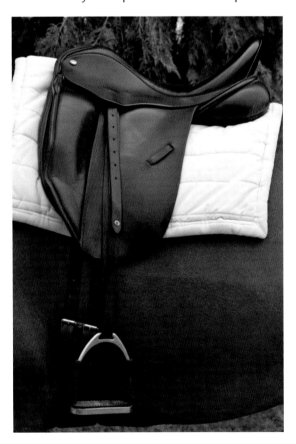

An example of a dressage saddle. (Photo: Oonagh McGibbon)

Another example of a dressage saddle.

the horse's back, and it is really important that the saddle design works for both horse and rider.

The middle of the seat of the saddle needs to be the deepest and flattest part so that the rider is centrally and securely seated; the pommel and cantle height ratio is relative to the particular discipline, whether dressage or jumping. A well fitted saddle enhances the freedom of the paces, increases gait symmetry, increases available power, reduces muscle soreness and damage, and increases performance ability. Obviously the reverse applies to a badly fitted saddle.

It has generally been accepted that the main pressure from a girth is on the sternum. However, it has now been established that the peak pressure zone is, in fact, just behind the point of the elbow, where girth galls are commonly found.

Modern thinking on girth design, taking this into consideration, is that the girth should be dramatically curved on its front edge to create much more room for the elbow and the bulk of the muscles in this area. This curve effectively guides the muscles back under the girth, rather than blocking them, thus reducing undue pressures and making it easier for the horse to use his elbows and shoulders more effectively. **But** it is very important that the girth fits very well and, in general, is part of a saddle/girth system, because the two elements will have been designed to work together.

There is often a noticeable increase in stride length in front and behind, and the whole horse benefits from the freedom such a girth allows.

Even the surfaces upon which the horse regularly works will have an effect on the pressures that build up under the saddle because of the loading on the horse's structure, so an even arena surface will be less disturbing than a hard road surface, for instance.

STIRRUPS

Stirrup length is more crucial than people often realize. If the stirrup length is too short the rider's knees are too high, the thighs become horizontal, the pelvis is tipped back and the rider tends either to lean back or collapse in the sternum. Exceptions could include a tall, long-legged person riding a small horse when shorter stirrups would allow for better application of the leg aids; someone with a long body and short legs; or when riding a young horse (for safety!).

Too long a stirrup length means that the hips are blocked and the rider tends to come into a fork seat, with the pelvis rotated forwards; this in turn brings the seat bones off the saddle as the rider stretches the foot down to reach for the stirrup irons.

LEFT: *Stirrup length too short, causing the rider to have a chair seat, and to be behind the movement. (Photo: Oonagh McGibbon)*

RIGHT: *Stirrups too long, causing a weak seat, and the rider to be easily unbalanced as he stretches down for the stirrup. (Photo: Oonagh McGibbon)*

Optimum stirrup length for balance and efficiency. (Photo: Oonagh McGibbon)

Stirrups are at the optimum length when the legs can hang freely and loosely down with the ball of the foot resting easily on the stirrup iron. Having the leathers equal in length on both sides of the saddle is a matter of management as mounting from one side only, usually the near side, will in time cause that leather to stretch and become uneven, with the result that the holes on that side will no longer correspond to the holes on the other leather. One obvious way of dealing with this is to change the leathers over regularly to maintain equal length; and even more to the point is to mount from a block of some sort, rather than from the ground, which has the added benefit of minimizing disturbance to the horse's posture and balance.

Obviously we are concerned here with dressage riders; jumpers of all persuasions have differently shaped and designed saddles to accommodate the necessary positions for jumping.

SHOEING

Farriery is a science but also an art; the farrier needs to have extensive knowledge of the overall anatomy of the horse, and in particular the bio-mechanics of the legs and the feet structures. Regular assessment of the way a horse moves is essential to the correct shoeing of any horse and, ideally, this assessment is made with it in hand and also under saddle. Balance is a word that cannot be used often enough in relation to horses and, to a large extent, their balance comes from healthy, equally balanced, correctly trimmed and shod feet. Computer-led gait analysis is commonplace these days, and farriers no longer have to rely solely on experience or guesswork to assess a particular horse's shoeing needs.

Manufacturers have come up with sophisticated remedial shoes for specific problems, but overall, shoeing comes down to the correct interpretation of the particular horse's weight-bearing when standing and loading when in motion. Riders have horses shod for grip, protection and support. Each equestrian discipline has different needs as far as shoeing goes, and in dressage we need shoes that allow a certain amount of slide on surfaces. Much research is now centred on the particular demands of dressage horses as the sport attracts more and more participation, and the financial implications require that each aspect of the horse's welfare is examined and solutions found.

This short chapter is just to flag up the importance of these subjects in relation to the general care of the horse, and the optimization of anything and everything that will help maximize its comfort and performance.

6 The Scales of Training

There is just as much horse sense as ever, but the horses have most of it.

Anon

The Scales of Training are the foundation stones or the building blocks of successful training: they are fundamental to any and all horse training. Given that the average horse is approximately 650-plus kilos of muscle and instinct, on what other basis are you going to ride safely?

Why are the Scales so important?

- Can you start, stop, halt square, turn left, turn right, go sideways, shorten and lengthen the stride within the paces easily?
- Is your horse obedient, light to your aids, does he work over a relaxed back into the rein, is he equally supple to both reins longitudinally and laterally, does he go sideways fluently, does he work with energy from behind?
- Is he a pleasure to ride and easy to control at all times?

What are the Scales?

Rhythm: Regularity. This is nothing to do with speed (tempo), it is the metronomic beat of each pace; some horses have a natural rhythm, others need help

Suppleness: Through the body – longitudinal; from side to side – lateral

Contact: From behind over the back to the hand – not pulled into a shape in front

Impulsion: Controlled forward energy, not speed; achieved through transitions

Straightness: Evenness into both reins and the hind feet stepping into and, when required, over the track of the forefeet and, ultimately, as a result of the preceding five steps.

Collection: the result of the correctly achieved previous scales.

Explanation

When the horse goes in **rhythm** with an even balanced pace (gait), relaxes over the back and is free of tension, with a swinging back, a lowered head and neck, and works willingly forwards, **suppleness** will have been achieved. When the horse seeks the rider's hand equally into both reins, responding to the rider's seat and leg aids, **contact** follows. He can them be ridden energetically forwards, (**impulsion** and **straightness**). When everything is in place, the horse will go in self-carriage and the long journey towards **collection** will be complete.

German is the language from which the English language *Scales of Training* is taken, hence the following translations.

Richtlinien is the generic term for the right lines, the principles of riding, using the Scales of Training, and the Scales are as follows:

Takt (rhythm/regularity);

Losgelassenheit (suppleness);
Anlehnung (contact);
Schwung (impulsion);
Geraderichten (straightness);
Versammlung (collection);
Durchlaessigkeit (throughness/submission).

The German word for self-carriage is *Aufrichtung*.

However, translation of these terms into one or two words absolutely does not work. For instance, *Schwung* encompasses swing, cadence, suppleness, balance, elasticity, elevation and ground cover.

As you can see in the Scales of Training pyramid diagram later in this chapter, the German terms go one stage further than ours, so collection is *Versammlung*, and the end product, so to speak, is *Durchlaessigkeit*. We translate this as throughness, submission and self-carriage.

Throughness is not an easy term to explain as it requires several qualities, all present at once:

- physical and mental relaxation and focus
- immediate responsiveness and submission to the rider's aids
- understanding and responding to half-halts
- sensitivity and light footedness
- in a correct rhythm
- in a consistent tempo
- cadence in trot and canter (a moment of suspension between each stride)
- walk should show activity and energy as there is no moment of suspension
- no hesitation, resistance, tension or stiffness
- connection from behind over a swinging back to a forward seeking contact

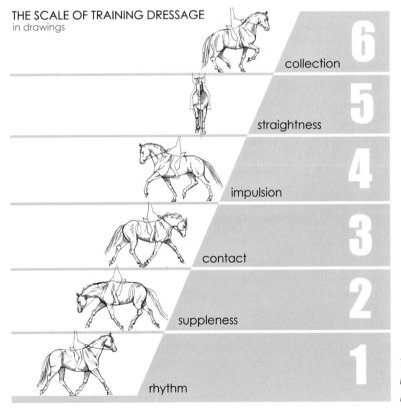

THE SCALE OF TRAINING DRESSAGE
in drawings

collection — 6
straightness — 5
impulsion — 4
contact — 3
suppleness — 2
rhythm — 1

The Scales of Training: the ladder of progression. (Diagram: Martyna Paczos)

- longitudinal and lateral suppleness
- forward energy with control
- straightness

However, '*throughness*' is a relative term as the degree of it will change, and it will become more established and improve with correct training from novice level through to Grand Prix.

The FEI directive for thoroughness is 'The supple, elastic, unblocked, connected state of the horse's musculature that permits an unrestricted flow of energy from back to front and front to back, which allows the aids/influences to freely *go through* to all parts of the horse.'

This simply means that the horse is through from behind to a submissive, elastic contact, bending round the rider's inside leg and into the outside rein, with support for the bend from the inside rein and control of the quarters from the outside leg. Consequently, the horse has equal weight over all four legs, he works with equal weight into both reins, and is balanced.

None of the exercises from novice to Grand Prix can be executed correctly if the horse is not working in this manner.

'Straightness' is an ongoing challenge throughout the training life of all horses, as they are not naturally straight. Generally, horses are almost always stiffer to one side, as indeed so are we, and this is something that needs to be addressed and readdressed constantly so that the power of the hindlegs can be properly engaged and used to the maximum (crookedness reduces the capacity of that power). The rider cannot force the horse to be straight. Systematic development of flexion on both reins ensures that the horse flexes to the inside rein when asked, in lateral work, turns and circles, and this helps with straightening; there is more on this in Chapter 8.

Crooked: quarters to the side, with the weight unevenly distributed on to the off-fore shoulder.

Crooked horses 'put' their riders in the most comfortable position for them, and this adds to the crookedness of both parties – often an outsider, presumably your trainer, will be able to see this clearly and will concentrate on re-establishing the straightness of both of you. Chapter 9 of *Understanding Dressage Training* covers this subject in depth.

Horses that have problems with piaffe, passage and the transitions between the two, and who make regular mistakes in the flying changes, commonly have problems with straightness – they swing their quarters, which makes engagement and weight carrying less effective. This should have been addressed much earlier in their training as it suggests that correct collection has not been established,

Submission: not submissive at all!

and more basic work needs to be undertaken to correct this as far as is possible.

The word 'submission' can also be somewhat of a problem in translation, as it is not intended to mean subjugating the will of the horse to the rider in any forceful manner, with over-strong rein aids – rather, it is the willingness of the horse to respond to the rider's sensitively applied aids with no hesitation or resistance, working over the back to a consistent, light contact.

Without rhythm, you do not have regularity, and you cannot have suppleness or a genuine contact: these three are crucial to the development of confidence and correctness. Without these three, you will not manage impulsion or straightness, and without all of these, true collection simply will not happen.

It is often debated, if not argued, that the Scales should each be more inclusive of the others, as practically they cannot be

Progressively submissive: Hayley using, in halt, just a light contact and a softly nudging leg aid.

as divided as a chapter such as this might suggest.

None of the six steps of the Scales of Training is intended to be taken in isolation: they overlap and are all part of the overall whole of training. Each step is crucial to the scaling of the pyramid.

These Scales are the concentrated result of many years of discussion, and the theory and practice of training horses by top international riders, trainers and judges. All training requires an obedient, malleable, flexible, willing horse to achieve the best results, and the maximum co-operation with the minimum of effort from you, the rider. (And, for sure, safe hacking also requires all these qualities.)

If only rhythm, suppleness, contact, impulsion, straightness and collection could become a mantra for dressage riders, trainers and judges, standards would improve and more horses would work through.

Jane Kidd

Every time you get on a horse, you train him whether you mean to or not – for every action there is a reaction according to science, so the practical application of these Scales of Training is of inestimable value to this end.

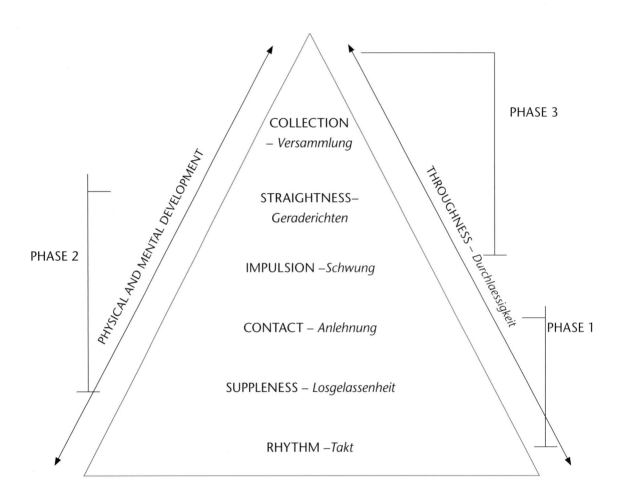

COLLECTION
– *Versammlung*

STRAIGHTNESS–
Geraderichten

IMPULSION –*Schwung*

CONTACT – *Anlehnung*

SUPPLENESS – *Losgelassenheit*

RHYTHM –*Takt*

PHASE 3

PHASE 2

PHASE 1

PHYSICAL AND MENTAL DEVELOPMENT

THROUGHNESS – *Durchlaessigkeit*

The Scales of Training pyramid: phases and overall aims.

7 Transitions, Half-Halts and Halts

Limitation is simply a perspective of mind.

Josiah Nicotra

A transition, according to the *Oxford English Dictionary*, 11th edition 2006, is 'the process of changing from one state or condition to another', and this certainly applies to transitions in dressage.

With young or inexperienced horses starting their education, transitions need to be judiciously placed and asked for, so that the horse keeps the forwardness and freedom without tension or anxiety – so some transitions, whether up or down, can be rather strong and forward going! The voice is an invaluable aid at this juncture, carrying on logically from the work on the ground. When riding still weak and unbalanced horses it is sensible to stick to progressive walk, trot, canter transitions as walk, canter, walk can put too much strain on such a horse's physique and can disturb the forwardness and balance in the transitions while the horse is still developing his strength.

Soon however, it is important to introduce the concept of the half-halt so that transitions can be regulated and controlled.

THE HALF-HALT

Half-halts are probably the most difficult, the least understood, the most mysterious and definitely the most valuable of all the training aids – and everyone is sure that they have the definitive version.

The clue is in the name – half-halt. So halfway to halt and then go. Another way to put it to the horse is to think 'halt, changed my mind, go'. A half-halt should take no longer to do than to say, so a count to three, or one or two strides, should be the maximum.

If the half-halt has not worked in this time frame, it has not worked. So stop it – and try again.

The definition from the FEI is as follows:

The half-halt is a hardly visible, almost simultaneously co-ordinated action of the seat, the legs and the hands of the rider, with the object of increasing the attention and balance of the horse before the execution of several movements or transitions to lesser or higher paces. In shifting slightly more weight on to the horse's quarters, the engagement of the hindlegs and the balance on the haunches are facilitated, for the benefit of the lightness of the forehand and the horse's balance as a whole.

Quite.

However, half-halts are unique to each rider and horse combination, and will change and be adapted to suit the situation on the day at the moment a half-halt is deemed necessary by the rider. The rider has to discover for himself the various nuances to be employed, by a mixture of experience and feel, as each horse will require a relevant half-halt according to what is happening. Sometimes the half-halt will be so subtle that only the horse and rider are conscious that it has happened; sometimes, however, less subtlety is called for and the resulting half-halt will be a very visible passive resistance from rider to horse.

Whatever the degree of half-halt, however, **the mantra remains the same – a count of three or one to two strides maximum**. Any more than that and the horse, being a creature that pushes against sustained pressure, will resist the half-halt and a pulling match will ensue – and we all know who will win that fight!

Riding is about forethought, analysis and feel.

Riders often leave horses to their own devices for too long so they get into their own bubble of rhythm and tempo, perhaps on to the forehand, and become slow, if not oblivious, to their riders' requests. The half-halt needs to be applied in the first stride when the rider feels that things are going wrong. This means that the rider must first of all be able to feel and follow the movement of the horse, breathing in a relaxed and calm fashion. Horses react to the feeling they receive from their riders, and shallow, quick breathing affects the rider's body and thus the horse. This, combined with an unyielding stiff position in the saddle, means that any attempt at half-halting is doomed to failure.

How to Ride a Half-halt

In a co-ordinated move, lengthen your legs and put some weight into the balls of your feet on the stirrup, without letting your heel drop (which allows your seat to come into play but not in a heavy way); at the same time, firm up your back and stomach muscles to momentarily resist the movement of the horse

whilst squeezing the reins (don't pull back). As you feel the horse respond and start to slow down, soften your spine and stomach muscles, release the weight in the stirrups, soften the contact and use your legs to send the horse forwards again. **Remember the three count rule**.

What does a half-halt do, and what is it for?

Half-halts, correctly delivered and received, *do* the following:

- re-balance the horse
- engage the horse's attention
- encourage more weight to be taken behind
- lighten the forehand
- lighten the contact
- make the horse more uphill
- refine the transitions
- alert the horse and prepare him for a change in pace, direction, frame and movement

Half-halts, correctly delivered and received, *are for* the following:

- as a communication tool
- as a support for the horse
- to enable the horse to become lighter and more submissive, and to work forwards into the contact, so that it is possible to shorten or lengthen his stride, as well as altering the frame up or down, at will while the horse keeps the fluency forwards throughout

That is a half-halt (or, at least, our version!).

Throughout the levels, half-halts increase in importance and frequency, helping to educate the horse and improve his balance, paces and expression. However, with Grand Prix horses, established in their self-carriage and content to remain in balance, the repetition of half-halts may well be confined to one before, one during and one after whatever movement, change of pace and tempo is required (this last thought is from Carl Hester in an interview with *Eurodressage* in 2013).

For other mortals, when half-halts are clearly understood and come through, then is the time to subtly employ more than one aid, as your horse needs to learn that although leg aids might mean forwards, this could be for a lengthened stride or for higher, more collected steps, rather than just fast forwards. The leg aids might mean stay forwards but also go sideways, or change legs in canter, or turn – or all of these. These aids all need to be broken down into their simplest form and then put together so that horse and rider are in tune. Ultimately, the rider must learn to use the aids with subtlety, and the horse should respond with a similar degree of subtlety.

MORE ON TRANSITIONS

Transitions are regularly said to be crucial to correct training and this is certainly true, although the number of transitions should be kept in proportion to the age and stage of training of the horse.

The point of the above detail in a book about advanced training is simply that, if these basics are not established and regularly reinforced, further training will inevitably be compromised.

Moving on in training, transitions are the way in which the horse is educated to collect and extend within a frame, without resistance. Try always to ride good transitions – and if it feels as if a transition is going wrong, abort, ride forwards and try again: transitions are the foundation of collection and extension, so particular attention needs to be paid to their execution. Good transitions are the results of successful half-halts.

It is important that a rider can ride the horse on straight lines, shortening and lengthening the strides at will, in all three paces: this is the hallmark of an advanced rider, and is more relevant than riding the more advanced movements for the sake of

*Halts: Olympic –
Kyra Kyrklund...*

Internationals – Pippa...

...and Hayley.

the movement rather than the improvement of the pace.

PRACTISING HALTS

Halts are very much transitions and, from a test perspective, the first and last impressions that are given to the judges. Halts work best when preceded by a shortening of whatever pace the horse is in (think of half-steps), keeping the horse coming forwards from behind and stepping into a momentarily restraining hand, which then allows the halt to come through to the contact. The horse should stay on the aids and be ready to go immediately forwards. Coming off the aids, having a good look round and losing focus should have been remedied early on in the training.

Square halts need to be taught and practised: they do not happen on their own, and the emphasis should always

be on a forward transition into halt. Any adjustments should be made forwards, even if it is a matter of having the horse move just one leg into place, never backwards. Arena mirrors are a huge help with this in the absence of a trainer on the ground. (Something as obvious as teaching your horse to halt square to be mounted or dismounted should not be overlooked.) In a test, high marks are reserved for halts where the horse is on the aids, equal into both reins, the front and hind legs are in line, the horse takes equal weight over all four legs and where, from the front and from the side, only two legs are visible.

As training progresses, it is almost impossible to do too many half-halts. Ask any top-level trainer or rider and they will tell you that they ride hundreds of half-halts, whether resulting in a noticeable transition, or something more subtle within a pace or a movement, as they are the basic requirement in bringing a horse to the top level of the sport.

ABOVE: *Into a square halt and straight move-off.*

LEFT: *How not to halt!*

8 Warm-up – Work – Cool Down

The biggest enemy to the partnership of dressage is impatience and the human nature to dominate other creatures.

Walter Zettl

Horses and riders are athletes, or need to become so, to deal with the physical and mental requirements of the more advanced work. As is well documented and scientifically backed up, a warm-up sequence, before doing more demanding work, is necessary to minimize injuries to any athlete, human or equine, and to prepare them for what is to come.

THE WARM-UP

It might sound ridiculously obvious, but the warm-up is literally time spent working the horse quietly to increase body temperature, allow blood vessels to widen and facilitate blood flow to the heart and other muscles,

allow more oxygen to flow from the lungs to the muscles, and give tendons and ligaments time to adjust to movement and improve their flexibility. It allows the horse's body time to warm up, and in so doing, gives the rider the same opportunity.

Depending on the weather and the time of year, it is a good idea to start the warm-up with the horse's loins covered with some sort of rug or exercise sheet and, indeed, the rider is highly likely to be similarly well covered at the start in a warm coat or jacket. Racehorses, for instance, are almost always ridden to the gallops for their daily exercise dressed in this way. It follows, therefore, that a warm-up in cold conditions would take longer than a warm-up in warmer weather, and ideally, the former would take advantage of any sun and the latter would take advantage of any shade.

The warm-up does not vary much for any level of horse because all the qualities required of a novice horse apply equally to an advanced horse – namely, that the paces are allowed to develop quietly, and that the horse lowers his head and neck while seeking the contact and stretching over the back.

The temptation with an advanced horse is to short circuit the warm-up and go straight into

Use an exercise sheet over the horse's loins at the start of the warm-up.

the more advanced movements. Do not go there – the relaxation and quiet development of the paces are just as necessary to the advanced horse, and perhaps even more so as he might well be older and stiffer.

Although one can make useful general points about the warm-up, each horse should have an individual warm-up that suits him. It is good to work out a routine, or programme, with which you both become familiar so that, in times of stress, you have something you can fall back on. This is particularly important with a tense, nervous horse.

Specific Warm-Up

Let the horse work quietly in walk for five to ten minutes, preferably on the buckle end if that is safe, so that the horse finds his own rhythm and natural balance (which you have disturbed by getting on him!). The walk is a really important pace, all the way to Grand Prix, and it is probably the easiest pace to spoil. The horse needs to learn to stride out in an active manner, moving freely in the shoulders and with an overtrack in all but collected walk. Thus, even though it is the relaxing pace a lot of the time, the horse should never be allowed to shuffle along but should always be encouraged to walk out. Generally speaking, riders take up the reins much too early, and sometimes this is because they need them for their own balance, so try not to allow this to happen.

If it is unsafe to start in this way, then it is better to keep a contact with as long a rein as you can allow and trot for ten minutes or so until you feel the rhythm settle and the relaxation that should come with that. Other horses may initially settle better in canter.

However you need to start, especially if in trot or canter, come back into walk as quickly as is feasible and let the horse walk on a long rein, into the contact. Keep the reins as long

Working quietly on the buckle end of the reins.

Relaxed and into the contact.

as possible and encourage him to seek and stay on the contact. Allowing him to wander around with his head in the air looking at everything will not relax him, nor will it make him concentrate on you and your aids. If he is spooky, flex his head away from whatever is taking his interest, moving his body in leg yield away from your inside leg and then ride him forwards into the contact again.

Take up trot and allow the horse to work in a slow-ish tempo while his muscles relax and he starts to work from behind with a rounded back. Use little half-halts to keep the balance and concentrate on the rhythm, staying on large curved lines, nothing too tight or too small. Ideally you would like him to work within a long frame, stretching towards the contact, trotting in a swinging, relaxed manner.

Some horses have good natural balance, others have to be taught to find and then stay in a good balance. The rider's task at any level is to find a balance that the horse can cope with at that time, and adjust it as the training progresses. Working too slowly causes problems because the horse is not able to work through his body, and too quick a tempo causes him to fall on to the forehand, flatten the paces and rely on the reins to

Hayley...

and Abi.

Stretching: Isabell Werth...

support his balance. So you are looking for a tempo that allows him to relax but is forward enough so that the rhythm can come through.

There is much said about stretching in the warm-up. In fact it is better just to allow the horse to work forwards into the reins, rather than insist on excessive stretching at the start, which is likely simply to send him on to his forehand. This is because the musculature is not yet ready and flexible enough to stretch; real stretching needs to wait until the muscles, tendons and ligaments are in working order, so to speak. As the warm-up progresses, he should come more and more into the contact, working from behind over a relaxed back.

When this has happened, start with trot, canter, trot transitions, adding just a little collection via half-halts, to test your weight and leg aids, and then send your horse forwards again. You should find that this is the time when you can give the reins even more forwards and have the horse follow the contact and work to it, without snatching at the reins. Repeat the above a few times until it becomes smooth and rhythmic. The horse's body position should not alter in the transitions or in trot and canter, and the whole upper line of his body should become loose and supple with this work.

Incorporate walk breaks into the warm-up so that the horse is not tired out before the real work starts. This all needs to be done on both reins to check that the horse is equally supple and loose, which, in turn, will help towards straightness – and it should not be forgotten that the rider's outside rein and leg support this exercise. The idea is that, eventually, the inside leg can take over the dominance of the inside rein to establish bend.

In Front of the Leg

All horses need to be in front of the leg. This is a much used and much misunderstood phrase, and this seems to be the right place to give you our explanation of what it really means and how it is achieved.

Briefly stated, your horse must immediately and enthusiastically respond to one light aid and stay energetically forwards in whatever pace you require until you tell him differently. It is not your responsibility to keep him active and forwards: it is his job to keep going under

his own steam without being constantly reminded by you.

This has several elements:

- you must be totally consistent and consequent about insisting that the horse always obeys your light aids
- your position needs to be sufficiently balanced and independent enough to apply those aids and deal with the consequences
- you should be able to keep your legs passively and lightly against the horse's ribcage when not giving an aid

The above are non-negotiable prerequisites, so that it looks as though the horse is performing of his own accord.

What does it feel like? The feel from the horse is that he works actively from behind, pushing the energy forwards under his centre of gravity, with corresponding freedom of the shoulders, so that you feel the whole body working as he takes you forwards. He lengthens his neck and stretches forwards to the bit, with a soft, light but definite contact, without resistance or tension. He is learning to propel, push himself from behind with engaged hindlegs, and this, ultimately, translates into the weight-carrying capacity of the hindlegs as he becomes more advanced and achieves self-carriage and collection.

The horse's temperament is an important consideration. Your goal in giving the aids is that you obtain the right reaction every time according to the horse's character. What would be a light aid for one horse might well be insufficient for another, so it is a question of finding out just how light your aid can become.

When a hot horse has learned to accept the aids, he can start to feel quite lazy! So it is important to recognize when you need to send this horse forwards again, and this time, in front of the leg and with tempo control.

A lazier horse will need to be ridden more

forwards and needs to learn to be quick and sharp off the leg. Rather than use a constantly nagging leg, use a short sharp kick once, or perhaps a tap of the whip, then allow him to go without further aids unless he slows down again, when you repeat the short, sharp leg or whip aid. Some horses will not react to the leg aid so a tap, harder or softer according to the reaction the horse gives, is a better option. Strictly done, this should have the desired effect and make him much more sensitive and reactive. Initially it might result in more forward movement than you anticipated, so be ready with a giving rein and do not get left behind when he surges forwards. Be sure that your correction has sufficient impact so that he really leaps forwards. Do not punish the horse for this: he did as he was asked, so reward his response!

Bring him back to the desired pace, be pleased that he is becoming reactive, and modify your aids accordingly.

Let him find his reward in the cessation of your forward aid and, since he will not know exactly when the next aid is coming, he should listen and react better to you. This method can be difficult for the rider psychologically, as it can feel as though you should keep giving an aid. However, this just makes sure that the horse learns to ignore you and becomes even duller.

Keep testing his reactions, and discipline yourself that you will never again use strong and constant aids. Your checklist is as follows:

- Give a light aid
- Evaluate the response – is it not good enough?

*How **not** to rein back!*

- Use a kick or a tap with the whip as necessary
- Re-test
- Evaluate the response – you need 100 per cent co-operation
- Praise

In the walk, he should go forwards with a light closing of both your legs on his sides – if not, see above. Then re-test – he should walk out immediately and actively. In trot, give a similar aid and expect a similar reaction. In canter, if he moves off a light aid and jumps up into the canter, the balance will be established from the first stride, engaging from behind and stretching into the contact.

Rein-back is a very telling exercise as it is regarded as a forwards movement. From a secure, balanced and square halt, the horse should step backwards from a forwards leg aid into the contact, to which he submits and reins back. Only a horse who is truly on the aids, and in front of the leg, will execute a correct rein-back with no hesitation, resistance or dragging of the feet, and he will be able to step up and forwards at any stage into whatever pace is required.

So, to conclude – a horse who is in front of the leg will allow you to refine your aids to the point where he stays on the aids on his own. Your rein aids are able to receive and control his energy from behind in a constantly recurring cycle, via half-halts, and the horse is connected from behind to the contact.

Being behind the leg is, obviously, the reverse of being in front of the leg. It feels as though you are sitting in a hollow, with one half of the horse in front of you and the other half behind you, with no feeling of connection or energy between the two. The horse either does not respond at all to forward driving aids, or runs away in front on to the forehand, becoming longer and flatter. This translates into the horse making the decisions as to whether or not he will go forwards, by how much and how fast. Not at all what is wanted at any stage!

Tempo Control

Tempo is defined as the speed of the rhythm: it has little to do with impulsion of itself, and you should always be aiming for something other than what the horse has offered so that you remain in charge. So, slow the trot if faster is offered, and vice versa. What works here is to adapt your rising to the rhythm and speed you require of your horse, so slow down or speed up your rising to regulate the tempo – in this way you should not need much rein. Half-halts and ensuring that the horse is in front of the leg are the two elements you need in conjunction with tempo control.

Vary the exercises to maintain or regain control over the tempo and the movement. Very often, a horse will speed up going on to the diagonal line in anticipation of a stronger trot or canter. In this case, it would be good to make a transition to a lesser pace, or collect within the pace, to re-establish tempo control, and then continue.

In general, ride a hot horse with tempo control first, so quite slow until he stays at the required speed by himself without rushing forwards. Hot horses often do not accept leg aids without over-reacting and trying to run away; however, they really do need to learn to accept the rider's leg otherwise more advanced work will be a real challenge. A good exercise is to go on to a smallish circle (12m) in walk, into shoulder-in on both reins, then into trot doing the same exercise, until the horse has accepted the leg and does not run away from the aids.

Warm-up Time

The length of time the warm-up takes will depend on various factors: the age, stage of training and temperament of the horse, the weather, the environment, your own stiffness – so anything from ten to forty minutes, with an ideal average of about twenty to twenty-five minutes.

The warm-up is not about the finished performance, it is all about quiet, calm work in a frame that allows the horse some freedom so his body and mind can come into a state where more concentrated work is possible. The paces should be even and regular but with little emphasis on expression or power – these can be developed in the work section.

THE WORK SESSION

Realistically it takes about four or five years, and often more than that when factoring in setbacks, time off and so on, to train a horse from novice to Grand Prix. Horses of eight or nine are capable of the Grand Prix work but will take several more seasons to become really confirmed in, and strong enough for, the work.

When the horse is experienced and confirmed at the top level, work sessions are more to do with using gymnastically suppling exercises than a total concentration on the actual Grand Prix movements, other than prior to a competition and even then, most of the top riders moderate the amount of collected movements they practise.

The first three elements of the Scales of Training are the ones to be concentrating on throughout all the work – rhythm (really this should be written RHYTHM) as it is so important, together with suppleness and contact. Impulsion, straightness and collection need constant and consistent thought BUT, without rhythm, nothing else works properly. It is about regularity, evenness, activity, elasticity, relaxation, tempo – the metronomic, rhythmic beat of whichever pace is being ridden.

What you should be thinking about all the time is ask (action), response (reaction) and reward (give the hand, stop the aid, stop the exercise, relax long and low), via half-halts of course. This phase is where you ride more specific movements from the level at which you are working, practise more direct transitions, and generally go through the work with the Scales of Training very much in mind.

Our experience is that work in canter at the beginning of the main work phase has several advantages. The horse is still fresh and can cope better with the tiring influence of canter and, secondly, the canter work is often beneficial to the forwardness and freedom of the subsequent trot work. So start with some canter, trot, canter transitions while you check on his response to your light aids, making sure he is steady to the contact and soft to the flexion and bend, so that he starts to take weight behind and comes more uphill.

Uprightness and Straightness

Together with the above, you need uprightness and straightness.

Uprightness simply means that the horse is through from behind to a secure contact, bending round the rider's inside leg and up into the outside rein, with support for the bend from the inside rein and control of the quarters from the outside leg, so that the horse has equal weight over all four legs and works equally into both reins, balanced and straight – not so simple!

Straightness versus Crookedness

On from this, riders need to pay more than lip service to the horse's inherent natural

*ABOVE: **Upright as opposed to leaning in: Grand Prix…***

*RIGHT: **…And four-year-old, showing the differing degrees of balance.***

crookedness. Loose in the field, horses neither bend nor are upright in motion. For instance, watch pretty much any horse coming towards you, or a racehorse coming down the straight towards the finish, and you will see four legs coming at you rather than the two you would see if the horse were straight (no one cares if a racehorse is straight or not!). So in other words, horses are naturally crooked and will revert to this state on their own.

Not straight.

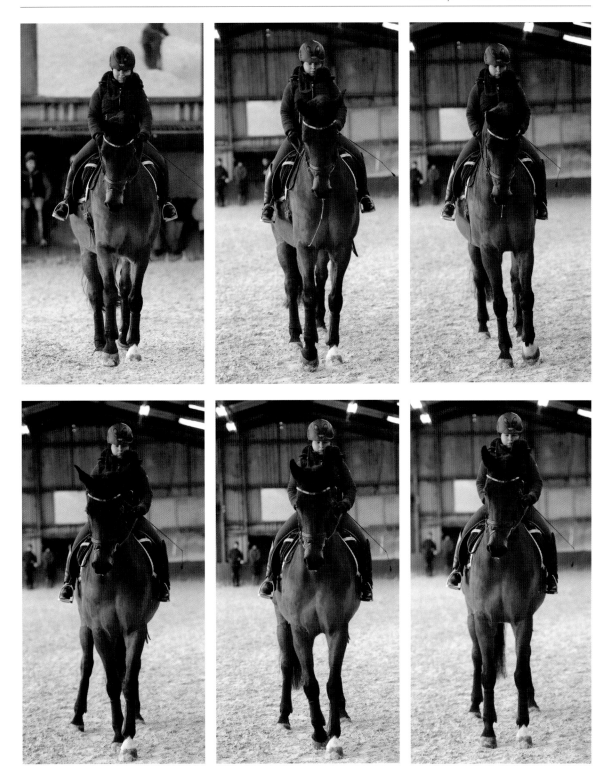

Not straight: contrived, but convincing.

Straight.

How does this translate into dressage training?

Crookedness is something for every rider to keep forever in the forefront of the mind. Close observation will tell you a particular horse's preference: some weight the inside foreleg/shoulder, others have a hindleg well out to the side and, indeed, most horses do both, left to themselves. Think about leading a horse – more often than not he will lean in towards you with his shoulder unless he has been trained not to do so. The perception that a horse is bent through his body often has more to do with neck bend created by the rider's hands than a slight curve from tail to poll in the direction of travel.

What to do?

The first thing is to recognize that this happens; and the second, obviously, is to do something constructive about it. This is not something confined to young, inexperienced or difficult horses – every horse in the world is prone to such a scenario.

Leg-yield in canter and counter canter are effective straightening exercises, and also build up fluency and elasticity. Check that you can stay straight on the long lines of the arena – this is when mirrors are such a boon, as you can check the straightness. If the latter is in doubt, first establish equal flexion to both reins, and then use shoulder-fore and shoulder-in to keep the positioning correct over the leading foreleg and to make sure the inside hindleg is coming sufficiently under the centre of gravity.

A universally used exercise is to ride a square of 15–18m – that is, four straight lines with four turns in between the straight lines – but in fact it turns out to be extremely difficult to execute this correctly. This is because the horse would rather fall in or out than go straight, and then in the turn he would rather put weight on the inside shoulder/leg, bear down on the inside rein, and probably also put the quarters to the outside – anything and everything other than to be straight and then bent.

As is often the case with new and difficult exercises, this is best done first of all in walk to establish first, curved turns, then 90-degree turns, and then quarter pirouettes in between the straight lines. Add a halt before each turn to set up the turn, and then ensure the horse is straight after the turn.

Done well, these squares are the acid test of uprightness, straightness and bend, and will render other advanced work easy by comparison.

Correct bend through turns and corners is only possible if the horse is upright.

This means taking the forehand slightly to the outside with the reins, using the inside leg and/or a tap of the whip to have the horse move his ribcage away from your leg, supported by the inside rein asking for flexion and the outside leg monitoring and controlling the hindquarters. You ask the horse to shift his weight off the inside foreleg/ shoulder and come upright into the outside rein. In fact, it should be possible to give the inside rein and still achieve correct bend.

Think constantly about a slight shoulder-fore so that you are always positioning the shoulders in front of the quarters.

These are the definitive exercises that improve the way of going and enable lateral work. If the horse is not straight and upright, the energy of the hindlegs is dissipated because the thrust from behind is effectively halved.

More Canter Work

Back to the canter work. With the horse now in a reasonable self-carriage so that he effectively canters on his own, the rider should be able to ask for the movements he wants to practise.

Correct bend through turns and corners.

- It is possible to do the square in canter. The four turns become quarter pirouettes: two or three strides of pirouette canter per turn, moving the shoulders in front of the quarters. Obviously, when the canter square is achieved, it can be made smaller and the quarter pirouettes then turned into half pirouettes, thus changing the rein. The latter is something to remember to do regularly with all exercises
- The final touch is that you check, from time to time, that you can ride this pirouette work with a giving inside rein so that the horse is working from your inside leg to the outside rein, keeping the bend.
- Ride some straight lines, not necessarily on the track, and ask for some shortened strides, into pirouette canter, and then ride on again. Do this on both reins, and quite often, so that this becomes easy and part of the everyday routine
- Ride on to a 20m circle with quarters in on to an 8m volte, keeping the rhythm and tempo intact without any variation – and ride out on to the larger circle again before he thinks of slowing down
- When this is easy on both reins, ride on to the short diagonal line, straight towards the centre line, set up the positioning, and ride a large working half-pirouette back to the track, staying in counter canter. At A or C ride a single flying change or perhaps a simple change, then ride the exercise again on the other rein

One half-pirouette is highly likely to be easier and more successful than the other, so you need to analyse the problem and come up with a solution.

- Is the canter quality good enough?
- Were you able to shorten the strides, keeping him forward and balanced?
- Were you thinking more about the movement than the pace?
- Was your horse straight and into both reins?
- Did you check the flexion and bend in preparation?
- Is he stiffer to one side than the other?
- Could you give the inside rein, and did he stay bent round your inside leg?
- Did you turn the shoulders round the haunches?
- Did you ask for too tight a turn?
- Did you ask for too many pirouettes and tire him out?

- Could you keep on the original line out and back?

You need positive answers or solutions to all these questions and should work on each aspect until the movement is equal on both reins, but not to the point where the horse is tired and stressed. There is always another day.

For some light relief, introduce some single changes at random around the arena, in between counter canter and simple changes, checking all the time that the canter remains forward and with enough quality to do good changes.

After a break, work again in trot and you should find that the horse is active and swinging through his body so that you can sit with ease. Bring him quietly into a little more collection by using some small half 10m circles, with a couple of straight strides and

Half-pirouettes: PSG canter half-pirouettes – three to four strides to the left and to the right.

Half-pirouettes: PSG canter half-pirouettes – three to four strides to the left and to the right.

Half-pirouettes: PSG canter half-pirouettes – three to four strides to the left and to the right.

Half-pirouettes: PSG canter half-pirouettes – three to four strides to the left and to the right.

a change of rein in the middle. Using weight aids via half-halts, step by step bring him more up together so that the trot starts to become more cadenced and expressive and he learns the very beginning of a few passage steps in a playful, easy manner.

Isabell Werth thinks that, *'Like children, they learn the easiest way when they are playing games. It's not always a game, but the horse has to enjoy it and think it's his choice to do the work.'* (*Dressage Today* forum).

The idea behind this work is that you can control him just with your seat (weight) aid which, in turn, should mean that you can shorten and lengthen the stride at will.

What is essential is that your horse should always wait for your aids and not anticipate. This becomes even more important the higher up the advanced ladder you go, as the horse does not know what is coming next, but hopefully you do!

A good way to finish this aspect of the work would be to collect him again and ask for some shorter steps, with a light tap of the whip if necessary, a few times and then let him work forwards/downwards into a longer frame, but still with an uphill tendency and definitely not leaning on the reins.

Leg-Yield

Take this feeling into leg-yield in trot, making the angles quite extreme to open up the shoulders and improve the quality of the crossing and the cadence. Without the bend required in lateral work, leg-yield can be used to great effect in this way.

Leg-yield: in-hand, learning to go sideways.

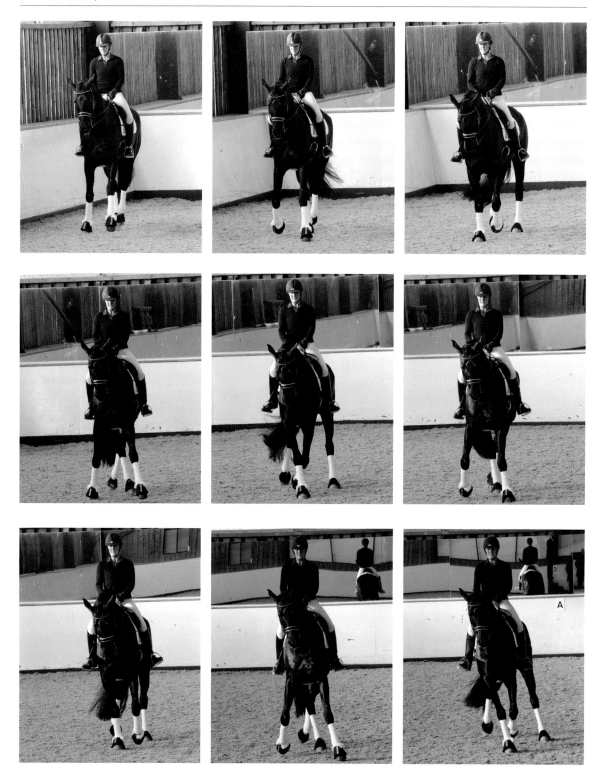

Leg-yield zig-zag.

Leg-yield zig-zag; note the flexion, not neck bend.

Then on into shoulder-in, renvers, travers and half-pass, often altering the length of the strides and the tempo within the movement. Check the self-carriage and contact by giving one or both reins from time to time and, after this collection, ride some medium and extended trot strides to make sure the balance is maintained and to freshen the pace.

Whatever the lateral exercise or pace, the rider should be able to ask for an immediate reaction to an aid which sends the horse into more extension, or brings him into collection, without hesitation. Extension comes from collection and both come from a judicious mix of lateral work, transitions to and from and within the paces, to build up the strength and stamina of the horse.

We are not advocating that all the above should be done every day, religiously. It is not necessary or desirable to train every exercise every day – you both need to stay happy and motivated – so it is better to choose just a few specific movements, interspersed by stretching and relaxation, which take the training forwards in a progressive manner but do not wear the horse out physically or mentally.

Lateral Work

Detailed explanations of the requirements of lateral work are available in *Understanding Dressage Training*, so we have used some sequence photographs to illustrate these movements, rather than repeat all the text. We have included renvers because, although it is not required in tests, it is a really useful exercise to test bend and flexibility, as well as placement of the shoulders and quarters. For a lot of horses lateral work in walk, without an over-restrictive hand, is an excellent way to introduce new exercises and to improve suppleness, and it can also be used to good effect with a stiffer, older horse.

Renvers to the right, hindlegs on the line, bent in the direction of travel.

Shoulder-in: on the left rein, from behind (the rider is compensating for loss of balance)...

...and from in front, bent away from the direction of travel.

Travers, or haunches-in on the right rein, preparation for half-pass; forelegs on the line.

Whatever the lateral exercise, flexion and bend are required, and the shoulders should always start the movement and remain in front of the quarters. Bend should be set up on the short side of the arena so that the following corner is ridden correctly and the shoulders are already well placed to start the exercise. It can be helpful to think about a shoulder-in position before half-pass, and this also deters the horse from falling into the half-pass with the quarters leading. **What is important is to finish the lateral exercise by straightening the horse, shoulders in front of quarters, before the turn or corner, so that you remain in control of the whole movement.**

Many advanced riders use shoulder-in specifically to improve hindleg engagement and to ensure that the horse is well and truly into both reins. One exercise which underlines just how much on the aids your horse is, and also how straight, is to ride on the centre or quarter line in shoulder-in, then, without deviating from the line, ride travers, then perhaps renvers, back into shoulder-in and straighten before the turn, making sure that it is the shoulders that you move and not the quarters. The quarters should stay on the line you designated when riding through the turn.

Shoulder-in is also most useful as an exercise when a horse is unwilling, hesitant or just misunderstands the aids to go from canter to trot immediately and hovers between the two paces. This can happen because, in advanced training, the usual transitions are canter to walk or halt, so the canter, trot transition can suddenly become an issue. Shoulder-in positioning on a smaller and smaller circle, until the horse more or less has to trot, is one way to resolve this.

Leg-yield, shoulder-in, renvers and travers need to be securely in place before working on half-pass because these exercises should have ensured that correct flexion, bend and sideways movement are in no way problematic to horse or rider. In particular, the rider should position the horse's shoulders correctly to start the exercises and then ensure that he himself is correctly positioned in the direction of movement so that the fluency is not compromised.

On the long diagonal, having established the correct bend through the short side and the corner, at the quarter marker take the horse first into shoulder-in and then into half-pass. If, as often happens, the bend is lost, then re-establish shoulder-in, and proceed again into half-pass. A variation on this exercise is to intersperse an 8–10m volte between shoulder-in and half-pass. In this way shoulder-in and half-pass can be ridden right across the diagonal to improve suppleness, bend and fluency.

The above leads the way into the more extreme angles and positioning in Grand Prix, where it is essential that the horse is laterally supple in order to cope with the steep angles and changes of bend, whether in trot or canter. Positioning within the half-pass, the ability to straighten and then re-position with the opposite bend, without over-shooting or under-shooting the markers, and while maintaining the quality of the pace, is what makes the advanced work strenuous.

Another useful exercise that combines lateral work with straightness and pirouettes is as follows:

- Start with alternating shoulder-in and travers on a 20m circle in trot; walk and ride forwards from the circle on to the long side
- Travers on to a small circle and ride a demi-pirouette back to the track, into renvers.

Through the corner and on to the centre line.

Half-pass: Grand Prix level – optimum crossing, excellent positioning.

Then give the reins and relax the horse for a few strides
- Into renvers again and, from that, push the shoulders back to the track and let the reins out again
- Take the reins up in walk, halt, walk on, then into travers into a pirouette, then halt – relax and reward

This is quite complicated, but it covers so many of the ingredients of advanced work and keeps everyone mentally occupied!

All this talk of collection, self-carriage, flexibility and athleticism leads one to think of extension. Many trainers keep the excesses of extension in check as they feel that too much extension work is hard on the horse's physique, and it is difficult to argue with that. However, simply put, impulsion and collection are the necessary prerequisites for extension, and alternating between the two furthers the horse's training and ability to respond to the rider's aids, as well as being a strengthening device for the advanced work. Too often one

Extended trot: Charlotte and Valegro...

Laura and Mistral Hojris...

sees horses with spectacular front leg action in the extensions but they are wide behind, so the hindlegs are not taking the necessary weight and the horse is, generally speaking, hollow.

The quality of collected work shows itself in the extensions, particularly in trot; it is strenuous for the horse to carry himself while covering the maximum amount of ground, whilst slightly stretching out his frame and swinging his back.

This latter sentence being a précis of Klaus Balkenhol's opinion.

Whatever happens, the aim should be to finish the whole session in good spirits so that the hard work culminates in a good result all round – even if this means that the work has not progressed quite to the level you had in mind. There is always another day, and what you have not achieved in forty-five or so minutes of work is probably best left for another time.

In any event, before the cool-down phase proper, finish the work on an easy note, doing something that both of you find stress free.

Hayley and WG Rubins Nite.

THE COOL-DOWN

This phase is as important as the warm-up.
Cooling down should just be a matter of long
and low, perhaps starting in canter but more
likely winding down in trot and then into walk,
on both reins, over a period of anything up to
about twenty minutes. It is during this phase
that the horse's body removes waste products
from the whole system, the muscles relax and
the heart rate gradually reduces to safe levels
– this can only happen if the horse is kept
moving for sufficient time to enable the body
to recover.

Basically, you want to take your horse
back to the stable in a relaxed, calm state,
breathing evenly, ready to be washed down,
rugged up and put away, or turned out,
depending upon the regime and the time of
day.

Just throwing the reins at a horse who
is sweating, breathing heavily and tense,
and putting him away in this condition, is
no way to treat any athlete at the end of a
work session and could put undue strain
on the horse's systems. If the session has
been stressful, there is even more reason to
cool him down sensibly. Sometimes a short
hack, perhaps round the edge of a field, or
a short session on the horse walker, might

The cool-down: stretching, relaxing.

be appropriate and, depending on the weather, an exercise sheet or rug should be used.

Both psychologically and physically, the cool-down phase is an important one for the minds and the muscles of both athletes.

WARM-UP AND COOL-DOWN AT A COMPETITION

It is much too late to be schooling movements at a competition – this work should have been done beforehand. The warm-up can follow a similar pattern to the routine you use at home, bearing in mind that horses vary in their confidence and concentration at shows. This could mean a longer and slower preparation or, conversely, something shorter and more focused; either way, the important thing is to find out what works best, by trial and error at competitions, so that you enter the arena warmed up, worked in, relaxed and controlled, but not tired out. Keep the horse moving just before the class – an active walk is fine – and pick him up a few moments before you are due in the arena. (Be ready to start when the signal is given; there is no 'right' to several turns around the outside of the arena, and you have only forty-five seconds from the signal to start the test.)

When the test is over, however it went, the horse needs to go through the familiar cool-down used at home so that he returns to his

Prize-giving: mounted – and exciting! WEG 2014.

stable, or lorry, breathing evenly with a normal body temperature and heart rate.

Mounted prize givings can be adrenalin making, to say the least, and you might have to go through a second cooling-down session afterwards!

Analysis of the test and how it went are an essential part of continuing improvement and education, but only after the horse has been cared for correctly.

Horses generally do their best to please us, but they do go how they are ridden, so it makes sense to ensure that we acknowledge that and ride accordingly.

9 Levels: Medium to Grand Prix

When you hurry a horse you just get to the wrong place faster.

Anon

British Dressage allows any and all combinations to compete up to, and including, Advanced. Above that – that is, for the FEI levels: PSG to Grand Prix – qualifying scores at Advanced are required (*see* the *Rule Book* for up-to-date information).

This means that anyone on any horse can compete up through the levels, and this is good as long as you are confident that 'having a go' will be a positive experience all round. There is nothing sadder, or more difficult to judge positively, than a combination well out of their comfort zone and struggling with the demands of the test. No one comes out of this scenario well.

In the UK, British Dressage currently offers restricted and open sections in all classes up to Advanced Medium, for which terms and conditions apply. Another option in the UK is to follow the Pet Plan route: this is a series of competitions currently up to and including Intermediare I, for which you qualify regionally, and then for the final at the Winter Championships. This caters in the main for the amateur owners/riders who feel too daunted, for whatever reason, to compete with riders at the Summer and Winter Regionals. Freestyle to music is also available at every level. However, as we write, the above is set to change in specifics as British Dressage has altered the competition structural ladder to accommodate members' wishes and concerns, so it is

obviously important to be *au fait* with what is offered, as it applies all the way to national Grand Prix. Full information is available in the Rule Book.

However, the general consensus is that you should compete at one, or even two, levels below that at which you are working on at home, so that you are both comfortable, and outside stresses and strains will not faze you.

Combinations should sensibly be gaining around the 70 per cent mark in the tests immediately below the 'new' level before going on up. Generally speaking, it takes about a year for most combinations to be working confidently with new exercises before moving up.

As with tests at all levels, it is the execution in rapid succession of the various movements that has been the undoing of many a combination. One way to discover how ready you are is to compete in music classes where you can make choices as to where and when you do the movements. And ride lots of tests at home so you and your horse become familiar with the pressure that riding through a whole test brings.

MEDIUM

There is a huge difference between a medium combination competing at the level, and a combination not yet ready for medium going through a medium test!

These days this level should be well within the reach of most combinations, as it is possible for riders to rise to the medium and extended trots (in the UK) and it is the first level at which lateral work is incorporated – shoulder-in, travers and half-pass (trot and canter) – the latter only at very shallow angles and on short lines.

Added to the work at the lower levels counter-canter, simple changes, walk pirouettes, rein-back to trot, canter to halt and halt to trot, medium trot to halt, are now included.

Within the paces more definition is demanded, so that all the trots – collected, working, medium and extended – have to be shown. The same applies to collected, medium and extended walk. All the canters – collected, working, medium and extended – are also required. In particular, the all-important transitions become even more crucial and must be demonstrated clearly and precisely for the higher marks.

The above requirements are designed to show off the level of training, the quality and fluency of the paces and the degree of self-carriage. Transitions and the smaller circles demanded are indicative, when well performed, that the combination is ready for the more advanced levels.

Worthy of note is that exercises should be accurate in terms of the exact lines. They must also start and finish precisely at the designated markers, and half-circles and circles should be of the correct dimensions (this is simple maths). A useful tip is to start an exercise as the rider's knee is at the relevant letter and should similarly finish when the rider's knee is at the letter that ends the exercise. It is worth pointing out that circles are devoid of straight lines and thus a circle will only be correct if it is circular! (Chapter 15 of

Understanding Dressage Training has all the information.)

ADVANCED MEDIUM

This entails the consolidation of the work at the previous levels. It also means single flying changes – although just because you have more or less mastered them does not necessarily mean that you are ready for Advanced Medium!

Any problems with rhythm, balance, suppleness and elasticity, contact, impulsion straightness and, to a degree, collection are going to be evident and will compromise a successful outcome. Give and retake in canter makes a renewed appearance, and altogether a much higher degree of self-carriage is required to cope with how quickly the movements follow one another.

ADVANCED

This level can be as demanding and challenging as PSG, with counter changes of hand in trot half-pass (zig-zag), 8m canter circles, 5m half-circles, and flying changes in sequence (three x 4s and three x 3s) added to the previous list.

FEI – NATIONAL AND INTERNATIONAL

This level includes PSG; Inter I; Inter A and B; Inter II; Grand Prix; and GP Special.

PSG: Requires five x 4s and five × 3s; the canter zig-zag with two half-passes; and canter half-pirouettes.

Inter I: Five × 3s and seven × 2s; full canter pirouettes.

Inter A and B: Seven × 2s and nine × 1s.

The big leap from PSG and Inter I to Inter II and Grand Prix is the introduction of piaffe and passage. Piaffe is undoubtedly the most demanding and difficult of the Grand Prix movements. The transitions into and out of piaffe and passage, and full pirouettes in canter, are the ultimate training objectives.

Inter II: Piaffe (eight to ten steps with 1m forwards); passage; transitions to and from piaffe and passage; seven × 2s; eleven × 1s; passage to extended walk; passage to halt.

Grand Prix and Grand Prix Special: Piaffe (twelve to fifteen steps on the spot); collected walk; passage to extended walk; nine × 2s; fifteen × 1s; canter zig-zag with five half-passes; and canter pirouettes on the centre line.

At each level, the movements in the lower level tests are included but with increased collection, self-carriage and degree of difficulty.

The FEI *Dressage Handbook – Guidelines for Judging* is a really excellent reference for finding out what is expected for every mark for every movement at every level. However, it is a dry read and probably not a book that one would be tempted to read through at one sitting. The British Dressage Rule Book has detailed definitions and explanations of

The FEI handbook: Guidelines for Dressage Judging.

the movements. For information on what is required at each level, it is necessary to study the particular test sheet (tests are updated regularly so be sure that the test you learn is the current one!).

However, in 2014/5 there are serious moves afoot internationally to codify each aspect of each movement and give it an individual mark so that a rider would know exactly which bit of what movement got what mark. This would apply at competitions worldwide, making the sport more transparent and the judging less subjective, according to the systems' supporters. At the time of writing this is still under discussion, but there is a strong move towards such codification.

10 Double Bridles

There are no bad bridles or bits, just the bad hands that use them.

Anon

This chapter is not intended to be an exhaustive treatise on bits, bitting and bridles – there is already a plethora of printed and digital information on the subject, and it seems unnecessary to reinvent this particular wheel. What interests us is how and why people use double bridles, and what considerations should be taken into account when contemplating their use.

Double bridles have been with us for centuries. They are mandatory for FEI competitions on the international stage. They are also allowed in BD national competitions from elementary level upwards, although these days it is possible to ride all the way through the levels to national Grand Prix using a snaffle bridle, with a couple of exceptions. Specific diagrams of permitted bits and text are laid out in the BD Rule Book and, doubtless, in other national federations' rule books. These are shown later in this chapter.

What is a double bridle? There are two bits in the horse's mouth, with accompanying extra leatherwork including two sets of reins, rather than one bit and one pair of reins. Properly fitted and expertly used the perceived wisdom is that the curb has one job and the bradoon (snaffle) has another job and, in combination,

Several examples of a double bridle; note the different nosebands and browbands.

the horse reacts to the differing pressures which allow the rein aids to be more sensitively and precisely refined.

Anyone who relies on the reins for their balance should not even consider the use of a double bridle. What is not acceptable is to use it as a means of applying the brakes – it will work in the short term, but will also contribute in time to a totally 'dead' mouth, and a rigid back and neck. Its efficacy will be much reduced and it does not solve the problem. Horses that are already heavy in the rein, or who tuck themselves behind the bit with their chin on their chest and a hollow back, will be even more likely to do so with a double.

Ideally, the snaffle bridle should be the bridle of choice when training, especially when new movements are introduced and/or the combination is going up a level. Then,

Double bridle is fine; hands are not fine.

Snaffle bridle with a padded noseband and a 'bling' browband with a curved middle.

when the double bridle is necessary or is deemed desirable, it is sensible to introduce the two bits but ride only on the bradoon to begin with, until the horse has learnt to cope with the extra metal in his mouth. Then, very carefully, introduce a light contact with the curb. If the curb chain is fitted correctly, the curb quickly comes into play and a giving hand is essential so that the horse doesn't feel trapped and, perhaps, rears or otherwise shows his dislike of the bridle. Already it seems clear that a rider contemplating using a double bridle should have a central, independent seat.

Another essential consideration is for the rider to become familiar and comfortable with holding two reins in each hand, and this is ideally done dismounted at the beginning. Putting two reins on a snaffle bridle can help, because it is really important that the rider can manipulate the two reins, gathering them up smoothly, easily and confidently, and not subjecting the horse to uncertain and incorrect rein contact.

Any training issues should be addressed before bringing a double bridle into the equation. It is, however, realistic to acknowledge that some horses do work better in a double because they have more respect for its action, and these tend to be horses who have, for whatever reason, had unfortunate beginnings in their training and have learnt to take hold in a snaffle. This is not to suggest, however, that this allows riders to make up for their own shortcomings by resorting to a double!

As an aside, it is really important to have your horse's teeth regularly checked, probably every six months, by a qualified equine dentist. A horse's teeth are designed to chew for the majority of each day, so in nature, the teeth are kept in shape. The teeth grow continually and the upper jaw is wider than the lower jaw so that they can grind efficiently. Horses chew in a side-to-side motion only possible when their heads are down in a natural grazing position. However, in the domestic situation, these natural practices are limited and they eat in a slightly different way so that hooks and sharp edges develop which, undetected and not dealt with, can cause severe damage to the cheeks. This inevitably causes pain and discomfort, particularly when a bit or bits are added, and what can seem to be deviant

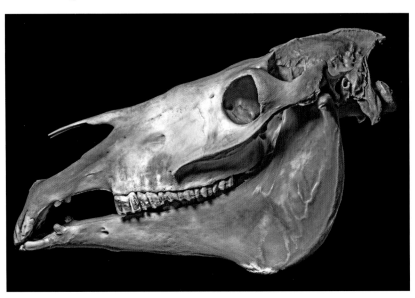

The horse's jaw, showing how the upper teeth protrude over the lower teeth.

or resistant behaviour is, in fact, an attempt by the horse to lessen the discomfort in his mouth.

The first considerations should be the size of the particular horse's mouth, the height of the palate, and the size of the tongue – these all affect the ability of the horse to accommodate the bits comfortably in his mouth.

What are the pressure points? There are seven:

- the poll
- the corners of the mouth
- the bars of the mouth
- the tongue
- the roof of the mouth
- the curb groove
- the nose

Depending upon the decisions made, the various pressure points will be more or less affected, and the horse may suffer unduly.

The bradoon: acts on the bars, corners and tongue. The effect is to raise the head via the corners, with an inward influence via the bars and tongue. The purpose of the bradoon is to regulate the horizontal flexion and bend, left and right, and it affects the forward energy (impulsion).

The curb: acts on the bars, tongue, roof of the mouth, curb groove and poll to increase flexion at the poll and influence the hindlegs. The curb bit, whether jointed, straight or curved, is not designed to be used to indicate bend. It is there for flexion at the poll, vertical flexion if you will, and the poll pressure asks the horse to raise the base of the neck and flex.

The noseband: Traditionally a cavesson noseband would be part of the double, and this still holds true; however, the fastening of the noseband is less straightforward and the

crank version is open to abuse as it can be tightened to extremes, putting far too much pressure on the nasal bones; padding can mitigate this as long as the noseband is fitted considerately.

These days bridles are often made with a cut-back headpiece to allow room for the ears, and they can also be padded to reduce pressure on the poll. Loose-fitting browbands can still do the job for which they were intended without being tight across the horse's forehead. There are already enough pressures on the horse's head just by putting on a bridle, without adding unnecessary ones, and research has shown that too much pressure on the nose, or on the poll, is undesirable and against the welfare of the horse.

It is important to remember that, just by the bits resting in the mouth, together with the weight of the leatherwork, the double bridle causes pressures even when not in active use. Some double bridles are really heavy just held in the hand – something to be considered before purchase.

Hands carried high and forward will increase the leverage and flexing action of the curb. When the reins are used in the default position, a rotation of the appropriate fingers and wrist will affect mainly the bradoon, leaving the curb pressure as it was.

FITTING A DOUBLE BRIDLE

The bradoon is fitted at the same height in the mouth as a normal snaffle, just causing a couple of wrinkles at the corners of the mouth. The curb is fitted very slightly lower with an angle at rest of 90 degrees, and when in use of 40–50 degrees, which is when the curb chain should come into contact with the curb groove.

PERMITTED BITS – BRITISH DRESSAGE RULE BOOK, 2015

Bits – Snaffles

Only bits following the configuration of those illustrated (below) are permitted. In doubt, guidance should be sought from the Sports Operations Manager of BD in writing with a diagram.

1. Loose ring snaffle
2. a, b, c Snaffle with jointed mouthpiece where middle piece should be rounded
3. Egg-butt snaffle
4. Racing snaffle D-ring
5. Egg-butt snaffle with cheeks
6. Loose ring snaffle with cheeks (Fulmer). **Fulmer keepers are permitted**
7. Snaffle with upper cheeks only
8. Hanging cheek snaffle
9. Straight bar snaffle. These must be straight and have no ports or raised bumps
10. Snaffle with rotating mouthpiece
11. Snaffle with rotating middle piece
12. Rotary bit with rotating middle piece

Bits of rubber, nylon or other synthetic materials are permitted. Bits must be used in their manufactured condition without addition to any part. Only the bits illustrated are permitted; mouthpieces may be used with any of the cheeks or rings illustrated. A mix of metals in the mouthpiece is permitted. A plastic snaffle with a cylindrical rotating mouthpiece is permitted. Minimum diameter of the mouthpiece is 10mm. Snaffles used in Young Horse classes must have a minimum diameter of 14mm.

Snaffles may be used at Advanced to Grand Prix including Premier Leagues unless a double bridle is requested by the selectors. Double bridles are to be used for all International FEI tests.

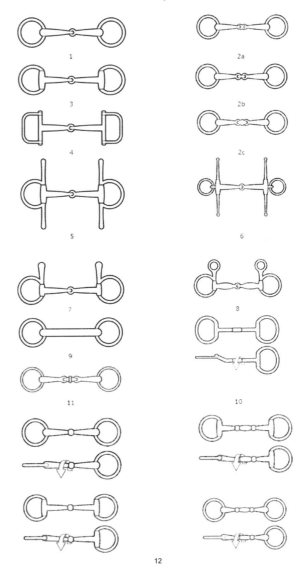

British Dressage rules: the snaffle bits allowed.

Bits – Double bridle

Bits should follow the configuration of those illustrated (below):

Bridoons:

1. Loose ring bridoon bit
2. a, b, c Bridoon bit with jointed mouthpiece where the middle piece should be rounded. Eggbutt sides are also allowed
2. d Bridoon but with rotating middle piece
2. e Bridoon Rotary bit with rotating middle piece

3. Egg-butt bridoon bit
4. Bridoon bit with hanging cheeks

Curbs:

5. Half-moon curb bits
6 & 7. Curb bit with straight cheeks and port
8. Curb bit with port and sliding mouthpiece (Weymouth). A curb bit with rotating lever arm is also allowed
9. Variation of bits No. 6, 7 and 8
10. Curb bit with S-curved cheeks
11. Curb chain (metal or leather or a combination)
12. Lip strap
13. Leather cover for curb chain
14. Rubber cover for curb chain

NB Curb chain hooks must not be fixed

Bits must be used in their manufactured condition without any addition to/on any part.

The lever arm of the curb is limited to 10cm in length (length below the mouthpiece). The upper cheek must not be longer than the lower cheek. The ring of the bridoon bit must not exceed 8cm in diameter. If the curb has a sliding mouthpiece, the lever arm of the curb bit below the mouthpiece should not measure more than 10cm when the mouthpiece is at the uppermost position. The diameter of the mouthpiece of the bridoon and / or curb must be such as not to hurt the horse.

Rigid bits coated in plastic are permissible in a double bridle however flexible rubber bits are not permissible.

The curb chain (including its cover) may be made of leather, metal, neoprene or rubber or a combination thereof and must be fitted in the conventional way.

Double bridles are compulsory for all Junior and Young Rider classes held at Premier League/High Profile shows (including U25 Championships) and at FEI International shows. See FEI rules for bits for U21 classes – www.fei.org. At all other British Dressage National shows where Junior and Young Rider classes are held snaffle bridles are allowed.

All competitors are advised to check their FEI Rule Book before taking part in a competition run under the FEI rules.

British Dressage rules: the curb bits allowed.

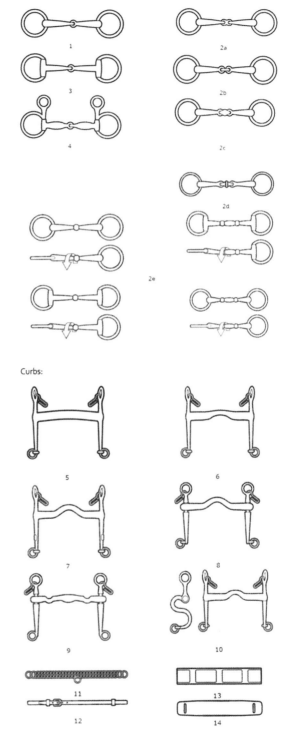

Curbs:

The curb chain should sit comfortably in the curb groove, and care needs to be taken that the chain does not twist or pinch this very sensitive area. It needs fitting with care so that it does actually lie in the groove, neither too high nor too low. Curb chains can be metal, usually stainless steel, thin or thick. They can also be metal encased in rubber or leather. Some metal chains, encased or otherwise, have a middle lower link through which a rounded leather lip strap can be inserted which helps to keep the bit from turning over in the horse's mouth and regulates the curb chain's position.

A curb chain fitted loosely is not kind, it is just incorrectly fitted, and it will adversely affect all the pressure points and change the effect of the bridle.

There is a huge range of curb bits and an equally large range of bradoons, not to mention the fact that there are different lengths of the curb-bit cheeks (shanks).

Thin versus thick doesn't always mean severe versus kind, as much depends on the available amount of room in the horse's mouth.

Some horses have a thicker tongue than others. Some have a lower palette than others, some have a narrow mouth, some have a wider one. For instance, a higher or lower port for the curb can help to alleviate undue pressure on the tongue, but care is needed that in so doing excess pressure is not transferred to the roof of the mouth.

It really is a question of trying several combinations, styles and sizes to arrive at the right one for your horse. Fitting requires experience and specialist knowledge so that all the above points are considered and the final choices are good ones. Then the bits need to be fitted in the correct position in the mouth, with the correct sizing for the horse, with the shanks an appropriate length (the length of the shank of the curb bit influences the severity of the leverage).

Inconsiderate use of the double bridle causes all sorts of evasions, in particular opening the mouth to escape the discomfort. A blue/purple tongue indicates too much pressure all round, and particularly, obviously, on the tongue. Horses learn to draw back their tongue or stick it out to the side, and they can get their tongue over the bits or even between the two bits. They cease to go forwards up into the bridle, or they draw their chin into their chest. In extremis, horses grab hold of the bits and take flight, whereas others rear at the slightest use of the curb.

In all these scenarios, the discomfort of the horse will be plain for all but the most obdurate to see. This generally suggests that either the bridle is incorrectly fitted, or it is just being used incorrectly.

DIFFERENT WAYS OF HOLDING THE REINS

There are several versions of how to hold the reins, and these positions exert various pressures. They range from what is mostly viewed as the default position, through to a method used very seldom outside strictly classical circles, and then only by very experienced riders. Pictures are often much better than words, so hopefully the following will prove useful.

The Crossed Method

Probably the default method and the one most commonly taught. The two left reins are held in the left hand and the two right ones in the right hand. The curb rein on both sides is the bottom rein. The bradoon rein is placed on the outside of the little finger, with the curb between the little and ring fingers, so that the loose ends of both reins come out between index and thumb, with the bradoon

Double bridle in use, the default method, the reins crossed.

Alternative method used by Carl Hester.

reins on top of the curb reins. This gives more emphasis to the use of the bradoon reins but it is possible to use the curb reins for extra refinement.

Alternatively the bradoon rein is placed between the little and ring fingers, with the curb rein between the ring and middle fingers. However, it is easy for the curb rein to be held too tight, sometimes without the rider noticing that this has happened, which suggests an indifference to the effect on the horse and inexperience in the correct use of the double bridle. Very often the curb and bradoon reins are held in a

fist, with both reins equally pulling at the horse. Keeping the curb reins about 1cm longer than the bradoon reins can help with this problem.

Parallel Reins or Uncrossed Method

The left reins are held in the left hand and the right ones in the right hand with the curb reins under the little finger and the bradoon reins between the little and ring fingers so that the reins are separated. This gives a degree of adjustability of the curb rein and also allows for the main contact to be on the bradoon. If the index finger is put between the two reins, this makes shortening either or both reins quick and efficient. (Hubertus Schmidt and Charlotte Dujardin use this method, with slight personal modifications.)

The above methods are the most popular and, in general, will be the ones most effective and easy for the rider to manipulate when necessary. The following two methods, whilst sometimes used by experienced riders

Parallel reins: Pippa Hutton; Charlotte Dujardin and Hubertus Schmidt also favour this method, with slight modifications.

searching for the best method for a particular horse, should not be lightly entertained by most riders.

The Fillis, or French, Method

The curb reins are held underneath the little or ring fingers, with the bradoon rein over the whole hand and held by the index finger, so a whole fist separates the reins. This can, in experienced hands, give the rider the flexibility to use the two reins for their separate purposes and can be useful in teaching a rider not to hang on to the curb during the more difficult exercises.

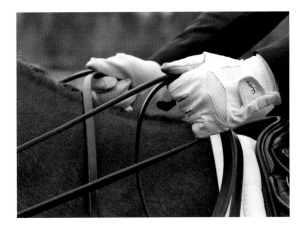

The Fillis or French method: a whole fist separates the reins.

The Three-and-One System

The right bradoon is held in the right hand, and all other reins are in the left hand, with the left bradoon rein under the little finger, the left curb rein above it between the little and ring fingers, with the right curb rein between the ring and middle fingers. Thus the left fist is stacked with reins and the right hand has just the one rein. It is very difficult to give fine aids with only

the curb reins; there can be a very subtle poll flexion but, effectively, the rider has to influence the horse through a totally independent seat. This method is deemed to be classical and is used at the Spanish Riding School in Vienna. It is not one for the average rider and is seldom seen outside that establishment! Its use stems from the historical tradition of fighting on horseback when the reins were held in one hand and the weapon of choice in the other.

The three-in-one method: the classical method, as used by the traditional riding masters and the Spanish School of Riding.

Quite a few riders like to just feel the little finger on the horse's withers, not leaning but just in touch, which they feel helps to keep a good connection with the horse. This also tends to keep the hands low and the elbows bent which should, in turn, help the rider to maintain a central and upright position. It is important that the rider holds the double bridle reins correctly so that the contact is even and secure: open fingers allow the reins to slip, with what can be adverse consequences.

All bits can be instruments of torture in the wrong hands, and the double bridle allows for infinitely more torture! As the quotation at the

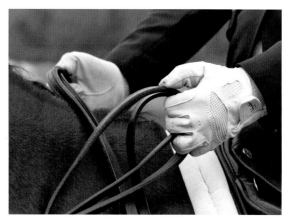

Holding the reins: fingers open, not so much gentle and giving as inefficient and insecure, with the thumb flat.

Holding the reins: correct, with fingers closed, the thumb making a small 'roof' to keep the feel secure yet light.

beginning of the chapter suggests, there are no bad bits or bridles, but there are certainly some severe ones.

The double bridle doubles the amount of damage that can be done to the horse's mouth, and is not something to use without good training, riding and plenty of thought behind it. When used with intelligence, integrity, in full knowledge of its capabilities and by someone with an independent seat, the double bridle can be most efficacious.

Incidentally, the tradition of passing left hand to left hand when meeting a rider going in the opposite direction hails from those days as the weapon was usually carried in the right hand. So left to left suggests a non-aggressive meeting and you should be very aware of the position of your dressage whip (especially with two reins)!

Finally, the FEI Rule Book has this to say about the acceptance of the bit/s:

> Submission does not mean subordination. The degree of submission is also demonstrated by the way the horse accepts the bit, with light and soft contact and a supple poll. Resistance or evasion of the athlete's hand, being either 'above the bit' or 'behind the bit' demonstrates lack of submission. The main contact with the horse's mouth must be through the snaffle bit.
>
> Article 416, para 2

(We take this to mean the use of the double bridle, where the bit is the curb and the snaffle is the bradoon.)

11 Flying Changes

Canter pirouettes are very often part of a sequence of movements that involve a flying change, which is why we have put this chapter on changes before the pirouette section.

Chapter 14 of *Understanding Dressage Training* does cover changes, but we felt that there is quite a bit more to be said on this subject.

Horses naturally perform changes when loose in the field, so it is not so much a matter of teaching horses how to change, but to change when we want them to do so.

The basic ability and understanding of changes from one lead to the other will have been taught at Advanced Medium level, if not quite a bit before that.

Young horses often offer a change if they find themselves unbalanced, and this can be quietly rewarded, before returning to whatever exercise was being undertaken, so that they are not punished for the change – later on you will need that inclination to change!

The main thing is not to cause anxiety and stress. If mistakes are made ignore them and ask again. Never punish incorrect changes, but just repeat, having made sure that the canter is sufficiently forwards and balanced, and that the flexion can be easily changed (*see* below).

The quality of the transition into canter is an indicator of the likely quality of the changes.
Stephen Clarke

PRELIMINARY EXERCISES TOWARDS CHANGES

First, ensure that the horse is quite clear about, and responds to, the aids to canter from walk. Then check that you can choose either right

Basic flying change: a single change of lead.

or left canter whenever you want to, and then add in simple changes. Chose random strides in between your canter, walk, canter – so five, or three, or eight strides of walk, then counter canter. Five, or three, or eight or two strides of canter, then walk, then immediately counter canter again, and so on until you can achieve one walk stride, then canter two or three strides, then walk one stride into counter canter.

Keep checking that the canter remains a true three-beat canter, with even, rhythmic, regular strides on both reins, balanced, not on the forehand or dipping downhill.

The horse needs to be able to stay in a shortened canter to achieve good changes. It is useful to counter canter against the wall or arena fence to teach your horse this shortened canter stride, as the wall keeps him straight and his hindleg underneath him, preventing him from stepping to the outside. Use the rein momentarily to reduce the tempo, while keeping him sufficiently forwards so that the strides shorten rather than slow. Repeat this exercise until you can ride a prescribed number of shorter strides without losing impulsion and jump, giving forwards again in between the working and shortened canters to check the forwardness.

The horse needs to be able to stay in this shortened canter, stretching towards the contact in a lowered frame and in balance. All this work should be done with light aids that elicit an immediate response, with the horse staying uphill and into a soft contact. Effectively, this is your own version of a 'changes' canter, not dissimilar to the 'pirouette' or shortened canter that is likely to have been part of your work programme already. This becomes the canter you need for teaching successful changes.

What one sees, too often, is a short, tight frame forced from the front, and the corresponding changes are short, choppy and lacking in forwardness and energy.

When riding counter canter, bear in mind that the bend over the leading leg should not be any greater than the bend would be in true canter. Excessive neck bend sends the quarters out, stiffens the horse through the back and makes changing legs correctly much more difficult. The purpose here is to alternate between counter canter and true canter as you achieve the shortened canter, so just a few strides of each. Endless counter canter will just tire the horse out without achieving the desired result.

However, it is also true that counter canter can be overdone, and this can cause your horse some confusion initially as, having learnt counter canter, he cannot believe that you are now suggesting that he should change legs back again!

Your horse should also be able to canter on a circle and remain in balance when you give the reins and allow him to stretch, changing the rein from time to time, and concentrating on an easy flexion to the inside. If the horse runs on to the hand, or loses balance, then use a smaller circle and give just the inside rein regularly until the horse obliges you by staying in balance and not changing tempo or rhythm. Then repeat on a larger circle until you are both confident in this exercise.

If there is undue stiffness on one rein, where the horse grabs hold of the bit on that side, some counter-flexion work is recommended. This involves riding, say, on the left rein in left canter, but with the horse flexed to the outside – that is, to the right – whilst maintaining a long, low outline. As you ask for this flexion with the outside rein, you also use your outside leg so that the horse goes into that rein and becomes submissive to that side. Repeat the exercise on the other rein – that is, right canter with left flexion – so that, in the end, you can flex your horse to the inside or to the outside regardless of the leading leg in the canter. This method should be used whenever you find your horse too much on your outside rein – that is, not equal into both reins.

This should make him much more even and elastic throughout his body, and ready to respond to the necessary flexion for correct changes. So, for instance, if in left canter, the horse will have left bend and flexion and should be positioned in a slight shoulder-fore. When you straighten him, prior to asking for a change of bend and flexion to the right, and/or a change to the right, he must wait for your leg aid and not change regardless.

When all the above can be achieved in a calm, consistent, relaxed manner on either rein, then it is likely that you are both ready for changes.

THE BASIC AIDS FOR FLYING CHANGES

The basic aids for flying changes are as follows:

- Half-halt, straighten, flex over the lead you require
- Move the outside leg back behind the girth
- Inside leg on the girth
- Support from the outside rein
- Apply the aids, using the outside leg to give the aid

However, some horses confuse the aids for travers, half-pass and canter, and with such a horse it can be clearer to use the inside leg to give the aid. Aids are just a matter of habituation and repetition, so once again, there is no right or wrong way to give the aids, just the way that is well understood.

Successful changes are dependent on the rider maintaining a central balanced position, as that will make a major difference to how easily and correctly your horse learns to change; so:

- Stay central in the saddle
- Do not throw yourself from side to side as this unbalances you both and increases the weight on the horse's front end, just when he needs that to be as light as possible
- Keep your upper body very slightly forward so you stay with the movement
- Keep a consistent contact and keep your horse's head and neck straight
- Do not block the change with an over-restrictive hand or heavy seat
- Half-halt, ask for a change of flexion, and use the clear canter aid with which the horse is familiar
- Do not suddenly over-do the canter aid
- Use your legs as if you are riding a bike (keep pedalling!)
- Do not clamp your legs on, rather keep them relaxed, so that they can swing easily
- Do not use your legs too far back, there is not time and you will be too late for the next change
- Learn to count canter strides, without changing: chanting out loud can help; feel each stride under your seat

When counting, what you will discover is that your balance has to be good enough so that you are in the right position to change your aids. The other thing you will discover is just how quick you have to be!

There are several methods of achieving the first flying change, and mostly, horses will offer a change to one side more easily than to the other, depending on their degree of stiffness and straightness (see above). It is not necessary to attempt to do changes to both sides too early on as this tends to cause tension. Stick to the one that seems to be the easiest, whether to the left or right – which is quite unimportant at this early stage. Horses often perfect a change to one side, whilst the other one takes more time and is often early in front or late behind.

Do not panic!

It is extremely counter-productive to punish incorrect changes and only has the effect of making both horse and rider anxious and tense, turning a mistake into a major catastrophe. These initial problems will usually resolve themselves in time if you have done the homework and kept calm and focused.

One thing to bear in mind is that horses can find doing flying changes either stressful or joyful. Either can mean that the horse takes off at speed after the change!

Whilst you do not want to stifle the exuberance, neither do you want to be out of control, so bring the horse back to walk as quickly and quietly as you can. Only repeat the changes for a limited time, perhaps three or four times initially, as part of the overall work, and perfect one change at a time. Whilst there is a tendency to congratulate yourself and your horse on the achievement of a good change, always remember that there will be something following on closely in a test, so self-congratulation must not interfere with what comes next!

The following are exercises for teaching changes:

- Ride a half circle back to the track in leg-yield, walk at the track with an immediate request for the new lead, and reduce the walk steps each time
- Ride a steep-angled leg-yield from the centre line to the track; on reaching the track, straighten, ride two strides of counter canter, then make a clear aid for the new canter lead
- Ride a short diagonal, M to E, in leg-yield in canter; at the quarter line, trot leg-yield to E, shoulder-in for two or three strides, pick up left canter; reduce the trot until it barely exists, and the horse should start to anticipate the new canter
- Ride two 20m half circles and ask for the change over X on a straight line with the new bend

- Come on to the centre line between G and C, or D and A, in half-pass and ask for the change as you position the horse for the new turn
- Use the short diagonal to keep the horse committed to the canter while the edge of the arena backs him off and helps with the change (David Hunt)
- Use the long diagonal to change the tempo and length of stride, shortening before the quarter marker and asking for a change into the new direction
- Work on a curved serpentine to keep the shoulders up and half-halt with the new outside hand as you give the leg aid (Nicky Barrett)
- Ride a small (8 or 10m) half circle back to the track and ask for a change just as you need to establish the new bend
- Ride counter canter-to-walk transitions, then counter canter on a large circle, riding in travers position, so in right counter canter the horse would be flexed left with the quarters to the left; then straighten and change (Carl Hester)
- Take up counter canter somewhere on the long side, and ride through the short side corner; as long as your horse is balanced and upright, ask for a change around A or C; done correctly this should help with collection and control
- Ride in counter canter across the long diagonal; just before the quarter marker half-halt and ask for a change just before straightening on to the track (the wall or arena marker should back the horse off and encourage a change)
- Ride forwards into the change and collect immediately afterwards (Carl Hester)
- Ride a four-loop canter serpentine, starting on the right rein; after the first loop push the quarters even more to the right (travers) and then, across the centre line, half-halt with the new outside rein (the right rein); change the flexion to the new soft inside

(left) rein; ask with the right leg for the left change

Each horse will favour a different method, and obviously, that is the one to use in the learning process.

Very often, horses swing their quarters out during a change. In this event, do as Carl Hester and his riders do and use the wall to keep the changes straighter. So, if the left change is crooked, ask for it from right canter so that the wall can help with the straightness, without much input from you. It really is important to make sure that both changes are 'clean' – that is, straight, forward and through from behind, before venturing into sequence changes.

Straightness is always an important consideration anyway, but particularly if you want to produce a series of sequence changes, equal to both sides, forward, expressive and powerful.

Apparently horses cannot count – well, we are not sure that that is entirely true! Initially anticipation is useful, but when the changes have been learnt, anticipation – not only of the changes, but also the sequences – often becomes an issue. So, make your changes in different places, on the long side, on the centre line, almost anywhere and everywhere except on the long diagonals initially, as this is usually where changes are done in tests. Also, make your sequences random, so that you stay in control of when, where and what.

This all matters, because at PSG, a single change comes after the half-pirouette but not until C. Another single change takes place on the centre line during the zig-zag. The sequence changes are on the diagonal, and there is also a single change just before the quarter marker after an extension.

So your horse really needs to wait and listen for the aids so that the changes remain under your control.

Having said all the above, however, it can sometimes be most useful for an established horse to be ridden through the test so that he does have an idea of what will be coming up, when – and then anticipation can be your friend.

SEQUENCE AND TEMPI CHANGES

These changes are a matter of:

- straightness
- good preparative work
- a quality uphill canter
- the ability to count
- good rhythm and appropriate tempo
- suppleness
- impulsion
- the willingness of the horse to wait for and obey your aids

Do not think of going on to sequence changes until you have fluent changes **on both reins**, whenever and wherever you want them. Then is the time to think about the next stage. Put some sequences together, but do not use precise numbers. Do a change, then a few strides, then another change, and so on – perhaps a change, then five strides, or six, or ten, it really does not matter. When this is relaxed and easy, and the way of going is as you want it, you can put more exact sequences together.

Riders often find four-time changes quite difficult to ride; perhaps luckily, they are only required at advanced and PSG levels, so they do have to be perfected – but if you have followed the previous advice, they should not be too much of a problem. Three-time changes are much easier, as somehow the rhythm seems to flow.

Remember that if you have too slow or short a canter you are making things unnecessarily difficult, as the shorter the canter, the shorter the moment of suspension, which is when and

where the horse changes leads – if in doubt, ride more forwards to give your horse time and room to change.

Do remember to take plenty of breaks, as this is strenuous work. Keep interspersing work on changes with true canter, lateral work and so on, to keep the forwardness and clear the mind.

And praise your horse for his efforts, as he needs to feel that he is doing well.

ONE-TIME CHANGES

One-time, or one-tempi, changes are when the horse changes the canter lead from stride to stride. The change of the leading front and hind legs takes place within the moment of

One-time changes: Grand Prix changes, fifteen one-time tempis.

suspension from one lead to the other. It is a prerequisite that the quality of the canter is good enough, sufficiently uphill and off the ground, and it should remain the same before, during and after the changes.

It is essential that the horse is very well

Three tempi changes: true, counter canter, true: left, right, left.

confirmed in the threes and twos before contemplating one-time changes. Most horses who understand these will cope quite well with a single pair of changes – that is, from counter canter to true canter. It can be most useful to set up a (very) quiet vocal signal to use in conjunction with these changes (but do not use the same signal as the one you already use, or will use, for piaffe).

If this goes well, a change from one side to the other and back, true/counter canter/ true, can be repeated a bit later on again in the canter work with the requisite praise and, probably, followed by either a more forward canter or even some walk and relaxation. This is something to repeat in a relaxed manner several times so that the horse becomes familiar with this new concept.

It can be very useful to do this in a larger space outside the size limitations of an arena, for instance in a field, where you are not constrained by a corner coming up – as long as you can maintain, or regain, control!

If the horse remains calm and the canter is forward and has some jump, next you try three or more changes – from true to counter canter to true canter – and always start with the change the horse finds the easiest. Progress is going to be related to the horse's temperament and the quality of the canter. If problems occur, or persist, then going back to what the horse finds uncomplicated is, in the longer term, the way forward. Tension and anxiety will cause uneven or incorrect changes and a loss of the forward energy and quality of the canter.

Less is more with the aids for one-time changes, which can be difficult for the rider to co-ordinate. The rider must be concerned with his own balance and keep a central quiet seat, with minimal aids, so that the horse's concentration is not disturbed. The more the one-time changes are established, the less you will need to move your legs and the more you can concentrate on keeping your horse forwards and straight.

One-time changes.

One-time changes.

One-time changes.

Riding a little more forwards in the changes can be helpful, and work on large curved lines can also be useful. It is essential that the rider keeps riding the changes forwards into the contact and does not over-restrict the front. Otherwise, what happens is that the horse might do the ones, but they will be short and choppy, lacking in impulsion and a forward, uphill tendency.

If the horse loses the cadence and collection, he is likely to throw in some two-time changes. Keep calm – do not slow down or speed up, keep the same rhythm and tempo – and try again. Better to go for fewer that come off, than insist on a specific number and cause the quality and calmness to be compromised.

As with everything, it is not so much that you can do them, but how they are done. Keep the rhythm of the changes in your head and in your body.

Normal canter transitions, forward and back, into and out of collection and extension, varying the tempo, the length of the strides and the ease of flexion left and right, should help to create and keep a more impulsive, uphill canter which will, in turn, help the changes. These established exercises can reassure the horse and restore calmness and relaxation.

Good one-tempi changes are forward, uphill and jumping through, free in the shoulders, fluent, rhythmic, impulsive, on the aids, expressive and ground covering, with the poll the highest point and the nose very slightly in front of the vertical.

ZIG-ZAGS

To give them their correct title, zig-zags are '*counter changes of hand*'. These movements require a specified number of canter half-pass strides, followed by a change of lead into the new direction, followed by half-pass, repeated a specific number of times, and a final change.

Depending on the level, this can be half-pass from a quarter marker to X, a change of lead, then half-pass back to the track (PSG) and another change; three half-passes 5m to either side of the centre line, with a change at each change of direction (Inter I and II); and at Grand Prix, five half-passes either side of the centre line with a change at each change of direction after three, then six, six, six and three strides, all to be fitted in between A and G. In the Grand Prix Special, only two half-passes are required, but the angles are steep (K to B and B to H), with a change at B and H.

Canter zig-zags at Grand Prix, starting with three steps from the centre line on the left rein ... 3/6/6/6/3.

... then change and six steps on the right rein ...

... change and six on the left ...

... change and six on the right ...

… and change and three on the left …

...finishing on the centre line on the right lead at G before C.

Jan Brink, Swedish former Olympian and world class trainer, suggests several exercises to help with the zig-zags, as follows:

● Shoulder-fore on the centre line, some strides of half-pass one way, shoulder-fore, half-pass back to the centre line, then shoulder-in. This exercise aids balance, control and suppleness, as well as establishing the straightness and immediate response to the aids; first done in trot and then in canter, with a change where necessary

● There is another exercise, done first in walk, which helps with the counting and also establishes just how far to go left and right in the Grand Prix zig-zag. What often happens is that riders go too far over one way, allowing the horse to drift through the outside shoulder, which makes it very difficult to achieve the change and get back across to the other side of the centre line. So, from D, three steps in half-pass, straighten, then six, six, six, and three to get back to the centre line in time for the final change at G. When this works in walk and trot, progress to canter, being very strict about the number of steps and, in particular, straightening and changing the bend before the changes

● Ride canter half-pass right, then into travers changing the bend, straighten into shoulder-fore to get the correct bend for the change, change, and then canter half-pass left, and repeat

● Out of the corner, ride five steps of half-pass, straighten for five straight strides; five in half-pass, straighten, and repeat. Shorten and lengthen the strides during the exercise to keep the rhythm, tempo and forwardness

The main purpose of all these exercises is to keep the quality of the canter, the straightness and suppleness, and to be able to control the number of strides and the accuracy. These exercises are strenuous for all concerned, so frequent breaks should always be incorporated for everyone's mental and physical wellbeing.

12 Pirouettes

Ride your horse calmly, forward and make him straight.

Steinbrecht (nineteenth century); adopted by Festerling, then Walter Zettl in his book Dressage in Harmony

A full canter pirouette is a 360-degree movement in canter on two tracks, with the radius equal to the horse's length and the forehand moving around the quarters – that is, the forelegs and the outside hindleg move around the inside hind. The latter goes up and down in the rhythm of the canter, not sideways, backwards or forwards, describing as small a circle as possible.

Half-pirouettes are ridden in walk and canter (and, in the Inter II and Grand Prix Freestyles, in piaffe and passage). The footfall must remain true to the pace, so in walk four-time and in canter three-time, with fluency and activity maintained. The walk half-pirouette is required up to PSG and the canter half-pirouette is introduced at PSG, following a half 5m circle at Advanced as preparation.

Pirouettes are covered in some detail in Chapter 5 of *Understanding Dressage Training*, so the following photographs should complement the explanations already given there.

Full canter pirouettes at Inter II and Grand Prix require an ability to collect and maintain balance without any sideways steps, with suppleness, rhythm and lightness of contact and the appropriate bend and flexion. A half-pirouette (180 degrees) should take three or four strides to complete.

Half-pirouette, as required for PSG.

Half-pirouette, as required for PSG: 180 degrees, three to four strides, to the left.

A full pirouette should take six to eight strides. Both require that the rhythm and quality of the canter is kept throughout the movement. It is also required that the line is maintained – that is, the line before and into the pirouette should be the line on to which the horse returns after the pirouette.

Full pirouette, as required for Grand Prix.

Full pirouette, as required for Grand Prix.

Full pirouette, as required for Grand Prix: 360 degrees, six to eight strides, to the right.

There has been extensive discussion, research and controversy about whether or not it is possible or desirable to maintain the three-beat within the pirouette. However, there is no argument that the canter into and out of it should be the same and should definitely be three-beat. Where the divergence occurs is whether or not the horse can perform the pirouette, more or less on the spot and on the hindlegs, without breaking the diagonal for an instant. Common sense (and the incontrovertible evidence of slow-motion video) dictates that this does happen.

A basic requirement for successful half or full canter pirouettes is the development of what is often termed a pirouette canter. This translates into a canter almost on the spot, with short elevated steps and a supple lateral bend, so that the horse can be turned, shoulders first, with ease. Practise this on straight lines first, for an increasing number of steps more or less in place, and then ride out, before thinking of adding the turns in a progressive way into smaller and smaller working pirouettes. Check the number of jump strides in the half and full pirouettes and, in training, vary them so that you keep control and can regulate these strides. If your horse starts to take over, use the outside rein and ride out of the turn – at any point – and start again.

Make sure that you sit centrally, and experiment with your weight to see where you need to sit to be the most help to your horse. A little more weight on the inside seat bone is good, and whilst you do need to follow the line of the pirouette with your body, do not over turn or you will lose the ability to support him with your inside leg and will adversely affect his balance, as you are likely to have slipped to the outside of the saddle.

Remember that successful pirouettes are exercises in strength. Through gymnastic preparation the horse learns to take weight behind, with his inside hindleg well underneath his body, so that he can maintain, on his own, the collection and balance required without depending on the reins for support. He needs to go off your inside leg, into the outside hand which supports him, with help from your passive outside leg. The shoulders are turned around the haunches, so too much outside leg is likely to cause the quarters to shift, with a consequent loss of balance. The inside rein indicates direction and bend, with the option of being able to release the contact so that he is not blocked by your hand.

One of Carl Hester's exercises is to ride canter half-pass into shoulder-fore into a working pirouette, riding the pirouette round an imaginary vertical pole (or person!) to keep it small, making sure that the shoulders are turned and that the hindquarters are kept under control via the rider's outside leg. This is very helpful as it stops you from asking for too tight a turn too early, which might result in a loss of footfall sequence and balance. Then it is important to move on into a refreshing canter to maintain or regain the quality of the pace.

The other major point is that the shoulders should be turned around the quarters, as already stated. This begs the question of whether, in training and in preparation, the quarters should be put into a travers position for the execution of the pirouette, and there are plenty of trainers and riders who use this exercise. The worry is that the quarters are displaced in the travers and this can lead to some sideways stepping

if the balance is not maintained correctly, because the inside hindleg that takes the weight in the pirouette is already to the side. Consequently, the shoulders will be less able to come round and it is easy to come off the line in the process.

Thinking about the first stride of the pirouette being in shoulder-fore position will keep the pirouette small at the start, with the shoulders leading, and then the focus can be on turning and riding the canter forward enough to keep the balance and impulsion. The maintenance of the quality of the canter is crucial – just slowing down with the resultant loss of energy and activity will not produce the self-carriage needed and the quality of the exercise will be poor.

Alois Podhajsky is in agreement with Hubertus Schmidt's contention that the pirouette should be performed from the shoulder-fore position as it keeps the horse straight and correctly positioned, so that the hindlegs can more easily keep the engagement and self-carriage required without moving out sideways. Hubertus is also adamant that the contact should be light and capable of being released even in mid-pirouette, just for a moment, to ease the horse's back and prevent him from coming too short in the neck.

It can be most useful to use the half-pirouette in walk to set up the half-pirouette in canter, going from one to the other without losing the line or the collection. If the horse understands piaffe, then piaffe into a canter pirouette and back into piaffe is a wonderful exercise for collection, strength and suppleness. These are exercises that some of the top riders, including Kyra Kyrklund and Jan Brink, use in training – and in freestyle tests to increase the degree of difficulty.

Whatever method of training is preferred, working pirouettes on a small circle (which progressively becomes smaller and smaller) will engage the hindlegs and teach the horse to carry more weight behind. This will lead to enough strength and stamina being developed so that the resulting pirouettes are correct, easy, and a pleasure to watch.

Keeping the horse in front of the leg, and waiting for the aids, is crucial as half or full pirouettes are always followed by another movement in quick succession, often a flying change. So there is no time for self-congratulation when the pirouette has been successful!

Pirouettes are mentally and physically taxing for both horse and rider, so this work is best done relatively early in a work session before fatigue sets in. Likewise, it is probably better not to follow one set of extreme exercises by another, even with an established Grand Prix horse, other than when practising for an upcoming competition.

13 Work In-Hand

One reason why birds and horses are happy is because they are not trying to impress other birds and horses.

Dale Carnegie

This chapter comes before piaffe and passage because it can be beneficial to teach the horse the rudiments of these exercises in-hand to help him understand what is required of him under saddle. This chapter is not an exhaustive treatise of all work in-hand, nor is it an extensive explanation of how to do it; this would make a book on its own and there are several already in publication.

In-hand work encompasses everything from the basic handling of a foal, breaking in the young horse, lungeing, driving, to therapeutic work when riding is not possible for either horse or rider, when time is short or because of injury – and advanced training up to Grand Prix.

Work from the ground, in-hand, either close up or from a distance of several metres, is an opportunity to observe your horse in a way simply not possible when riding, for obvious reasons. The purpose is to see how he moves, how he reacts, whether he is tense or calm, lazy or hot, supple or stiff, and what makes him anxious or relaxed, and how he communicates with you.

It can be a lesson in itself, or simply be used to remove the excesses of energy before climbing on board. It can be most useful for a lazy horse who can be made more active and forward thinking or, conversely, for an excitable, anxious horse who needs to be calmed down.

Our focus in this book is on the work in-hand that can enhance and improve a

horse's way of going and education, and this includes some unmounted flexion work, using either the snaffle bridle or the double bridle, which can then also be done under saddle. This is a much neglected area of expertise these days, although in earlier times the Riding Masters used it as a matter of course, as they found it to be beneficial to horses working at all levels – and our experience is that there is definitely a place for such work for various reasons with different horses.

Some studies have been done in Germany which looked at the correlation between tension and work in-hand. Horses worked in-hand before being ridden had a lower heart rate than horses who were not worked in-hand. This was a side result of some research looking at rein length and tension, but it was clear in all the results. The question is, of course, why would this be?

Some possibilities were suggested:

- Perhaps the horses trained in-hand were more relaxed because their trainers were more relaxed
- Perhaps the trainers were more focused on taking their time to train the horses, and were not as goal orientated as their riding counterparts
- Perhaps the trainers were more educated about the need for a horse to be in balance: physical balance equals emotional or mental balance for horse and rider

- Perhaps a horse trained in-hand is more likely to understand the trainer's body language, because he can see the trainer
- Perhaps the horse becomes familiar with the required responses to aids given by the trainer, which then translate more easily into ridden aids, because the neural pathways have been set up

Food for thought.

Obviously, horses learn to be handled in the stable, and when being led, rugged up and so on. Early work preparatory to breaking in a young horse is done quite close to the horse, sometimes with two people, so that the horse can understand what is required, and then he is taught to lunge in all three paces, on both reins – this takes time, patience and expertise, but is outside the scope of this book; there are many useful books that go into the necessary detail.

Work in-hand teaches basic patterns of walk, trot, canter, halt, turning round, going backwards, standing still, using body language and verbal cues. You can teach sideways movement, bend and flexion, how to give in the poll and jaw (flexion), how to wear a bridle without fussing in the mouth.

Ultimately, you can teach all the Grand Prix movements without ever actually getting on the horse, if that is your interest. Like riding, however, these techniques take time, experience and feel to acquire before such heights can be reached. In-hand work is not to be undertaken lightly by an inexperienced horseman: it is difficult to do well, and habits formed by wrong training in-hand can be very tiresome to correct later on.

We have been very lucky to write this chapter in conjunction with David Pincus, whose biography can be found at the end of this book. He is one of very few exponents of this art in the UK who is able to show the work we have just described with a variety of horses – including Sally Shetland!

EQUIPMENT

The equipment required ranges from the very basic to the quite complex.

Some people prefer to lunge off a cavesson noseband, especially made for lungeing, in conjunction with side-reins and a saddle or roller.

Others lunge off a snaffle bridle, either directly from the inside ring of the bit, or through the inside ring to the outside ring, or by clipping the lunge line to the outside ring and passing the line over the horse's head and through the inside ring, from inside to outside and thence to the trainer's hand – again with side-reins. These three methods are best left to experienced trainers who will know which method is appropriate, when and why.

Some trainers use a snaffle bridle underneath a cavesson.

A lunge cavesson is suitable for most work. There are pros and cons to each method, but all should be used with knowledge of what the pressures and influences are on the horse.

Generally, however, lungeing off a headcollar without any side-reins is an exercise without control, or hope of control, and teaches the horse little or nothing in the way of improvement or obedience.

There are lungeing rollers with rings placed at various levels on each side, through which the lunge line can be threaded, depending into which outline one intends to work the horse (high, middle and low), and which do not require the horse to wear a saddle. Others will use a saddle with a surcingle over it to keep it and the stirrups in place, using the stirrup leathers in place of the rings mentioned earlier. This may sometimes be practical and a shortcut if time is short, but a roller with side-reins would be optimum. Most methods require side-reins of some design or another, which are attached from

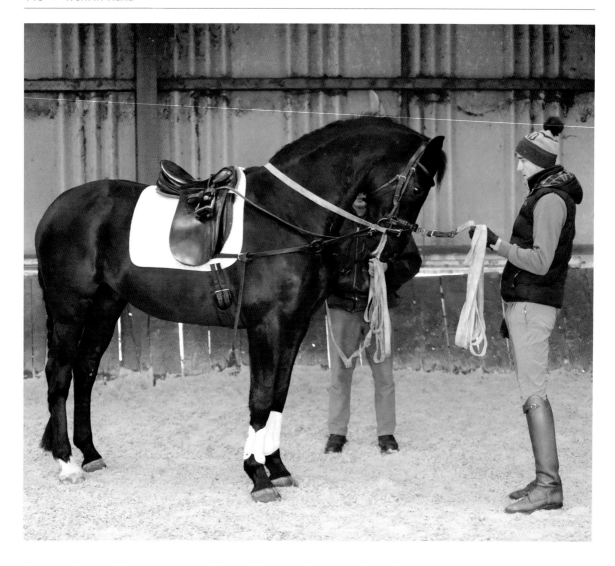

Horse equipped with a cavesson, snaffle, saddle and side-reins, with two handlers.

the bit rings on both sides to a ring on the training roller or surcingle. How loose or tight these side-reins are set will depend upon the age and stage of training of the horse, and the work that it is intended to do with him.

Each trainer has a favourite way of attaching and using all the equipment. Whilst the individual choice of equipment is too complex to discuss here, it is recommended that gloves are worn, as well as sensible footwear and clothing that cannot get caught up in the

equipment or flap about. Brushing boots on all four of the horse's legs for protection are a sensible precaution, as would be over-reach boots, and a numnah or saddle cloth under the saddle or roller.

For more advanced work, on the short reins or when working directly behind the horse with double reins, the tail is often bandaged and caught up, or plaited, to minimize the risk of it catching in the lunge line or the whip.

Horse in a snaffle only, boots all round, but no other tack.

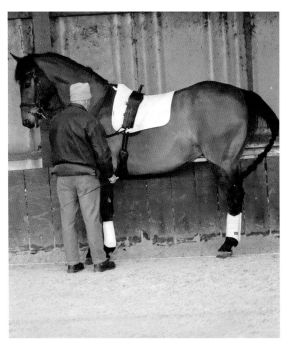

In a snaffle; also wearing a roller, numnah, side-reins and boots.

Ridden in a snaffle: Advanced...

...and Novice.

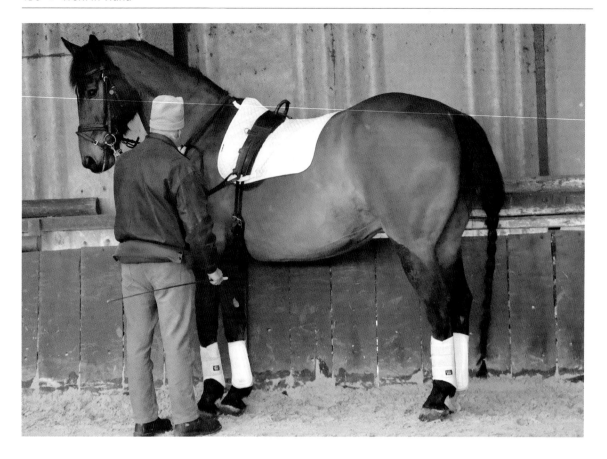

Plaited tail.

Double bridle, boots and over-reach boots.

Lunge reins typically allow a lunge circle of between 15 and 18m, and the best are made of double thickness lightweight webbing, with a swivel fitting at the attachment end. A lunge whip of 1.5–2m in length with a good light balance in the hand is essential.

It is a good idea to work with the horse to familiarize him with the whip so that he is not nervous or over-reactive. He needs to have respect for the whip but should not fear it. Teach him to accept the touch of the whip all over his body and neck – this takes time and patience but is well worthwhile. This applies equally to the long lunge whip and to the shorter whip that one would use for closer work.

This does, of course, have the added advantage that the horse is likely to work more confidently when ridden with a whip.

Lars Petersen at the Global Dressage Forum in 2014 with Allan Gron on Zick Flower (six-year-old by Zack X Romanov): early stages!

Lars Petersen and Allan Gron: early stages!

Care is needed to begin with as the horse can, and often does, over-react and might kick out from fright at something unexpected happening behind him or from a general fear of the whip (see above). Whilst the occasional kick is reasonable and understandable, this reaction should not be allowed to get out of hand, and a sharp half-halt on the rein from the handler might be necessary, and/or sending the horse backwards and then forwards, which might well solve the problem. If your horse reacts in an extreme way and lunges forwards, the best way to deal with this is to turn him on a small circle and re-present him again.

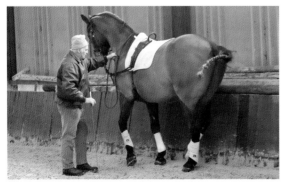

Circling round to regain control and calm; then re-presenting.

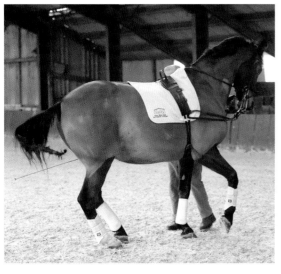

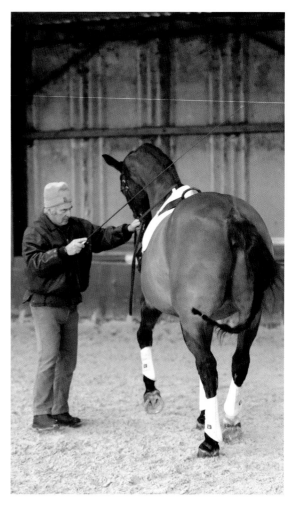

Where to touch: using the whip, often just pointing, at the hindleg, the croup, and above the hock.

All whip work requires common sense and care so that violent reactions are reduced to the minimum and no one gets hurt.

Initial work in-hand with a whip either just above the coronary band, where horses are often most sensitive, on the lower hindlegs, above the hocks or on the croup, or even just tapping the arena floor, can give the horse a good start. Every horse will be different, and it is a matter of trial and error to find the most effective spot to touch the horse with the whip.

Work with two lunge reins has the advantage that the trainer has better control of the horse's quarters and can work the horse into both reins, which aids the horse to work on a single track with some bend and without the quarters falling out of the circle. Half-halts and transitions become smoother and, of course, this is closer to what will happen under the rider. The smaller the circle, the more engaged the horse needs to be which, in time, develops more strength and collection – but, as ever, this needs to be done judiciously. It is also possible to change the rein in a figure-of-eight pattern without stopping the horse; this requires some clear signals from the trainer, patience, and a certain amount of dexterity.

When the horse has two handlers, one has the rein on the cavesson to control the forward movement, while the other, usually the trainer, has control of the lines on the bit rings and works by the side of the inside shoulder or hindleg, the reins in one hand and a shorter whip in the other (the lunge whip is too long and unwieldy for this work). Having already been familiarized with the whip, it is then used to tap one leg at a time and hope that the horse responds by lifting that leg. The point is to encourage the horse to use the tapped leg to step more under and engage.

With two people and two reins, the work can now progress to piaffe in-hand. With the side-reins attached, the trainer takes the outside lunge line over the withers into his hand; the handler controls the forward movement with a lead rein on the cavesson, in conjunction with half-halts from the trainer. Then, with light taps of the whip on the hindlegs, alternately, in the place you have already found to be the most effective, ask for a reaction: the horse should lift the leg and put it down again. Praise. Gradually, this develops into half-steps with a very small amount of forward movement, regulated by the handler and the trainer. Be content with a few willingly offered half-steps, and then walk out. Repeat, but as ever, do not be over-ambitious and take your time.

When this is all established, the trainer can work alone, with side-reins fixed appropriately and holding the cavesson or snaffle rein, walking backwards at the horse's shoulder, giving half-halts and using the whip – one person, one rein. The whip is no longer just used to indicate a leg, it can now be used on the shoulder, on the quarters, on the croup, at the girth, anywhere that needs a correction or response.

SPANISH WALK

As mentioned briefly in the section on passage (see the next chapter), teaching a horse Spanish walk can improve the freedom of the shoulders and, with some horses, this can be most beneficial. Good hand-to-eye co-ordination is necessary, and this is a skilled operation, not for novices!

First, teach your horse to pick up a leg by tapping just below the knee, on the cannon bone, with a schooling whip – not hard but sufficient to cause a reaction. When the horse picks up the leg, stop tapping and give a titbit. Standing at the shoulder, out of harm's way, you should be able to reach both feet, so do this exercise alternately, praising and treating every time. Reaction = titbit (piece of carrot, apple or horse cube). Progressively ask, by tapping again, that they should reach the leg out a little further. Reward each reach. Quite quickly, this can turn into a strike out forward with the leg, up to the height at which you hold the whip, so the higher the whip the higher the leg will reach. Do not get in the way!

As the photographs show, the horse will eventually lift and stretch the leg out in quite an extreme fashion – and yes, this is what you want; this is likely to take several days to achieve, always keeping in mind that the horse should stay calm and relaxed. A session of

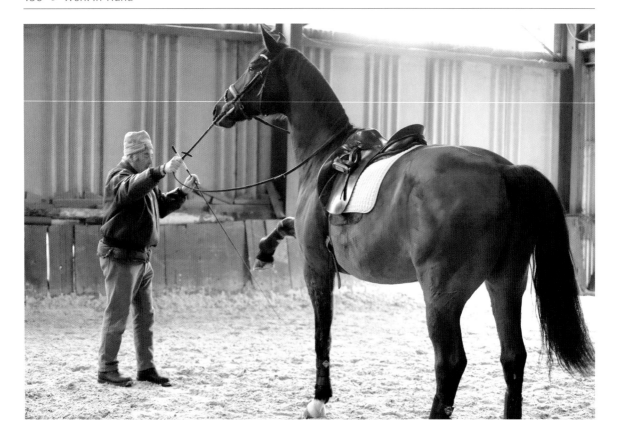

Spanish walk: in-hand...

fifteen minutes or so is quite sufficient; time enough to teach, but not so much time that the horse becomes fractious.

Next, you want the horse to move forwards as well as lifting each leg alternately; just give a forward indication with the reins and use a voice command if you like – 'Walk on'. Reward the smallest attempt. Give a titbit every couple of strides forwards as long as the horse also stretches up and out with the forelegs. By this time you should only need to point the whip at the leg you want him to use.

Make sure that you only reward positive reactions, and then only when you have actually asked for such a reaction. Your horse should never demand a titbit, he needs to earn it, so ignore any unwarranted

leg raising. You do not want to create a horse that paws the ground. **A warning here: do not randomly wave a whip at the front end of any horse who has learnt Spanish walk as they will, naturally enough, react.**

Under saddle, you should be able to touch the shoulder with the whip and 'cue' the reaction. If this does not work at the beginning, have someone on the ground to help.

This can be a fun exercise with a serious point, but do **make sure the horse is confirmed in piaffe** before attempting Spanish walk.

The balance and engagement required are the same for in-hand work and work under saddle, but for the horse it can be beneficial

...and ridden.

not to have the rider's weight on his back when he is still learning what is required. Equally, it is very instructive for the trainer to be able to observe how the horse is using himself.

Work in-hand from the ground, without a rider, is more often than not followed by work in-hand with a rider. Ultimately, the rider can work alone without help from the ground, once the horse has thoroughly understood the exercises and the transference of aids from the trainer to the rider is complete.

Size is not an issue! Little...

...and large.

14 Piaffe and Passage

The stride can only be as long as the horse's neck is long.

Anon

GENERAL POINTS

The two exercises of piaffe and passage, plus canter pirouettes, constitute the highest degree of collection and difficulty in dressage. All the Scales of Training must be in place, and, as Hubertus Schmidt says: 'In every situation in the high collection, you must be able to stretch them – 90 per cent of horses are too short and the rider cannot make them longer or deeper.'

All the textbooks and rule books state that the poll should be the highest point, but this is not always totally achievable, especially with a stallion who has a big crest. However, what is important is that the horse should be on the aids, through and over the back into a submissive, light contact, uphill and not deep or behind the vertical. Being able to count all the plaits as the horse comes towards you suggests that he definitely does not have his poll as the highest point!

Piaffe and passage are forms of trot where the legs are seen to work in diagonal pairs. This seems to be universally agreed, but what is still a subject for debate, in spite of technological advances in slow-motion camera work, is whether or not there is a moment of suspension in both. From this research, it is pretty clear that passage has the longest moment of suspension of all the trots – thus there is definitely a moment of suspension in passage.

In piaffe, for the horse to transfer the activity and spring from one set of diagonal legs to the other without forward movement, there has to be a moment, albeit extremely brief, where this change of loading takes place. Whether, because of its brevity, it can truly be called a moment of suspension is less clear cut, and expert opinion is divided. If everything about the piaffe is correctly presented, then there can be a difference of execution between one horse and another, where one horse has more natural elevation, spring and impulsion than the other. The raising of the forehand is relative to the increased bend in the hindquarters of a particular horse, and must remain so.

Without such qualities, the piaffe deteriorates into something more akin to a shuffle than a trot.

There will, of course, be a considerable difference in the piaffe and passage shown by a horse at the beginning of his Grand Prix career and that shown by a horse that is established and experienced at the level. The differences will be further emphasized by the individual horse's technique and conformation.

Ideally, piaffe is shown on the spot, or almost, its elevation and cadence due to the transference of a forwards intention into an upwards one, whilst keeping the desire to move forwards. This is essential for its own quality, and also because it is so often ridden

World class: Carl.

On the way: working well towards piaffe.

in conjunction with transitions into and out of passage. One could say that piaffe and passage are as much about the transitions between the two as they are individual exercises, as the better the transitions, the better the exercises.

Both movements require considerable engagement of the hindlegs, a lowering of the croup, and a clear flexion of the lower leg joints, and the horse should exhibit excellent balance, lightness of the forehand and a corresponding lightness of the contact, rhythm, straightness, elasticity and throughness. They demonstrate the progressive development of weight-carrying strength in the hindlegs, longitudinal and lateral suppleness, and self-carriage in an advanced outline without hollowness, with the poll the highest point.

The rider who has arrived at the stage where these exercises are about to be taught to the horse should, ideally, have learnt the

Schoolmaster in piaffe.

feel of piaffe and passage on a schoolmaster so that the timing of the aids can be established. Some horses undoubtedly have more aptitude for these movements than others – for instance, the Iberian horses and Lipizzaners – but a few lessons on a seasoned Grand Prix campaigner should be sufficient for the purpose. These horses are few and far between, but it is possible to find them if you are sufficiently determined.

The most difficult aspects of this work are the transitions into and out of each movement, keeping the activity, balance and elevation while achieving fluent, smooth transitions. This is yet another reason to experience these exercises on a schoolmaster.

PIAFFE

Generally, piaffe is more often taught before passage, but as always with horses, there will be exceptions when a horse is not naturally forward thinking, or lacks some impulsion, and then the passage can help to establish the necessary energy.

Riders and trainers vary in their approach to this work. Some prefer to work in-hand, while others prefer to work from the saddle, often with someone on the ground at the beginning, and yet others combine these methods.

Isabell Werth, the multi-Olympian for Germany, used always to train her horses in piaffe and passage from trot, from the saddle. However, she now works with a Spanish trainer, José Antonio García Mena, and the initial work is usually done from the ground

in-hand, first in walk and then in trot, before trying the ridden exercises. Klaus Balkenhol, Arthur Kottas, Kyra Kyrklund, David Pincus and other world class trainers also use in-hand work first without a rider, and then with a rider, before completing the transfer of the aids direct to the rider.

These days, sadly, it is the case that fewer trainers have the knowledge and experience to train piaffe successfully from the ground. As a result, some horses who have difficulty with the movement, and especially the ridden concept, never learn to piaffe correctly. In-hand work, correctly executed, is still a very valuable way of training and should not be lightly dismissed. This is why we have devoted a whole chapter to this way of working horses, as it is one of Angela's main interests and something she uses regularly in her training.

Whether in-hand or from the saddle, the horse needs to be totally responsive to half-halts and capable of frequent transitions on and back within the trot and particularly from trot to walk to trot to walk, that are **straight, engaged and immediate**, before attempting piaffe. Horses that are not on the aids, and through, will struggle to cope with the demands of this exercise.

Beginnings: trying hard to understand.

Having said that, piaffe is not something only to be introduced to advanced horses!

Half-steps in walk should be second nature to a younger or inexperienced horse as part of the strengthening and engaging process so that, in conjunction with half-halts, these 'baby piaffe' steps are in place from an early stage and are not a worry for the horse.

Setting up a vocal 'trigger' – a click or other similar noise used only for this purpose – is very useful in the early stages and throughout the training. Then, as the horse works out what is required and offers even a step or two of what is, initially, a jog, the reward should be praise and walking forwards out of the half-steps. Over the months, this is repeated until the horse voluntarily offers some short elevated steps as he obeys the familiar half-halts and voice aid. These transitions, done correctly, improve the contact and close the horse up from behind, so that the rider can influence the hindlegs and achieve the necessary throughness.

The first piaffe steps will not greatly resemble the end product, and each horse will have his own rate of progress, achieved by patient, calm, progressive development. What is clear is that this work takes time and patience.

It is important to stress that each horse should be worked as above in-hand and/ or under the saddle according to his temperament and the way in which he learns most easily; there are no fixed rules.

The Aids for Piaffe

To give the aids for piaffe, the rider:

- sits evenly on both seat bones
- keeps a soft seat
- maintains an upright position with the legs at the girth
- gives the leg aids alternately, or both together in rhythm (see below)
- maintains a quiet, elastic contact, via half-halts

The quieter the aids the better, the aim being to aid the horse into the movement without disturbing his balance or equilibrium, with reins that contain the horse but allow the movement to stay forwards in front of the rider's leg.

It is not the job of the rider to do the piaffe for the horse, which is too often seen!

Some trainers do not advocate alternate aids as they feel that this can encourage the horse to swing and, in addition, great sensitivity from the rider is necessary for such aids so that the horse is not distracted or confused. It is also true that the aids for trot and passage would be given with both legs together. Internationally, it is certainly more common to see both legs used in this way. It is impossible to be totally prescriptive here as the aids you use will depend upon what works best for you and your horse.

It is best not to rely on the whip for piaffe for two reasons: the first is that the horse should have learnt the movement willingly and without the need for strong reinforcement from the whip; and the second is that whips are not permitted under FEI rules.

Spurs, which are mandatory at this level, are there to be used as precision tools – to activate and engage the hindlegs to keep the horse in the two-beat rhythm; they are not there to force the movement.

Piaffe has the possibility that the horse will become excited and over-anxious because of the amount of impulsion required, without the freedom that forward momentum would allow, so it is really important to keep the horse relaxed, focused and balanced. Time is what is required for the horse to learn piaffe, and also then to perform it.

A hurried, stiff-legged, resistant piaffe is no piaffe at all.

Carl remarks, 'Nothing becomes supple unless you bend it, flex it and move it.'

Exercises for Piaffe Under Saddle

The following exercises may be used for piaffe under saddle:

- Cavaletti – work over poles and then cavaletti is quite a fun way for horse and rider to develop the necessary lift and flexibility in the joints before embarking on more serious piaffe work
- Lateral movements – shoulder-in, travers and renvers in walk and trot – on both reins, are excellent preparation for piaffe as they cause the respective inside hindleg to carry more weight and to step underneath the body
- Changing the tempo and shortening the trot should create lift and suspension in the trot
- Add transitions between walk, trot, halt, trot, shoulder-in and rein-back, all done without hesitation and with the horse moving between the exercises with only the slightest leg aid as the horse becomes gymnastic and flexible

This work, combined with the half-steps already learnt, means that you should be able to ride collected trot to walk to trot to walk, with the horse reacting to the driving (leg) aids and restraining (rein) aids very quickly. More often than not, this work results in a few jogging steps into the walk – the whole point of the exercise – and a reaction deserving of praise.

The following exercises may also be useful:

- Ride on to a 20m circle in walk, in shoulder-fore position, asking for a few short steps behind that will resemble jogging steps, and then walk again, being very quick to praise even the smallest positive response. Repeat this several times until the horse understands what is required. Quite often a light tap with a whip will help this process
- Ride small circles, progressively down to 8m voltes, in walk, which help the horse to learn to take more weight behind and sit with a lowered croup, whilst keeping the strides even in length, height, tempo and rhythm, as the circles diminish in size. The walk must remain active, calm and forward. If any tension, anxiety or resistance creeps in, then walk on into a larger circle before trying to shorten the strides again
- Ride a collected trot in a straight line, against the wall, then collect even more for just a few strides, no more than three or four, then ride forwards into collected trot. The trot strides should be active and into the contact so that the rider can easily ask, via half-halts, for what is effectively a less forward trot, without losing energy. Do not, at this point, think about piaffe: think only about shortening the length of stride in the trot before trotting on. Repeat and reward as above
- Carl Hester is an advocate of working in rising trot in the initial stages of piaffe work, as this can reduce the pressure on the horse's back at a stage when the back is not yet strong; it also helps to keep the rhythm constant
- Ride a collected canter into some piaffe steps, and then on again into canter. This exercise requires that the horse has some experience with what is known as pirouette canter and half-steps, so that he will be familiar with the concept of both and can keep the fluency forwards in the transitions from canter into the half-steps and on into canter

All these exercises are strenuous for the horse, requiring both strength and

concentration, and are not successful or consistent in five minutes.

The Finished Article

The FEI definition states that:

> The height of the toe on the raised foreleg should be level with the middle of the cannon bone of the other supporting foreleg. The toe of the raised hind foot should reach just above the fetlock joint of the other supporting hindleg.

The above definition is quite brief, so it would seem to be a good idea to expand on the above definition:

- The forearms should be parallel to the ground with the toe of each foreleg raised to the middle of the cannon, and with the toe of each hindleg raised to the other fetlock
- The forelegs, from the knee down, should be vertical
- The quarters should be lowered, through compression of the hindleg joints, so that they come well under the centre of gravity and take the weight behind.
- Horses on the forehand usually piaffe too high behind because their balance is too much over the forelegs, even if they are moving forwards
- The neck should be raised and arched, in an advanced frame, without hollowness and with the poll the highest point
- The horse should also be light in the hand with the nose slightly in front of the vertical
- The requirement is, eventually, for between ten and fifteen steps of piaffe, depending upon the test being ridden
- In addition, the horse should be absolutely straight and the piaffe must keep the forward tendency so that a transition into an expressive, elevated passage can be achieved immediately without hollowing, loss of suspension or cadence

What one wants to see is:

- an athletic, gymnastic movement involving the whole of the horse's body (back mover) and not just the legs (leg mover)
- a light, rhythmic footfall, equal on both diagonals, forward-thinking, easy-looking, cadenced, with no hesitation or resistance
- quick-reacting, sensitive, sharp, gymnastic exercises, without tightness or mental tension
- the ability to go into, and come out of the piaffe, without hesitation or resistance

What is often seen is a horse that:

- hollows behind the saddle and is inactive behind
- is high and short in the neck
- is too deep and behind the vertical
- is against the rein and heavy in the hand
- steps too much forwards
- has the forelegs too much behind the shoulders
- just shuffles the forelegs up and down, with too much weight over the forelegs
- is over-engaged, with the frame too closed so he gets stuck behind and cannot easily come out of the movement
- is wide behind
- swings behind or lifts the legs in an unnatural or exaggerated way
- has a varying rhythm
- has a varying tempo
- shows tension, anxiety and resistance

The difficulty of the piaffe is not only in the balance for horse and rider, but it also requires complete concentration and the building of strength. The horse needs to gain enormous control of his body, combining aptitude and ability with a willingness to perform.

Grand Prix: piaffe (twelve to fifteen steps in competition).

Grand Prix: piaffe (twelve to fifteen steps in competition).

A finished piaffe gives the impression of remaining on the spot, with the hindlegs bending in all the joints and stepping underneath the body. Then the raised hindleg comes vertically under the hip, the croup lowers, the shoulders lift, the back is supple and supporting, the forearms are almost horizontal, with the diagonals in perfect symmetry and rhythm. The energy and elevation give the piaffe its elegance.

Interestingly, the European preoccupation over the last few years has been with young horse classes and the necessity of producing spectacular forward paces in order to showcase and sell such horses. Collection and work towards piaffe, with the self-carriage necessary for it, has been somewhat neglected, and it is only relatively recently that this has been acknowledged and steps have now been taken to remedy the situation.

PASSAGE

General Points

Passage is a collected yet forward-moving, uphill cadenced trot, full of energy and elevation and with a long moment of suspension as the horse springs from one diagonal set of legs to the other one. It is at this point that it will become crystal clear whether or not the basic training, refined by many hundreds of transitions, is adequate to the task.

As with piaffe, transitions within trot, including into medium and extended trot from collection, together with lateral exercises to improve the carrying power of the horse, are part of the necessary process for passage under saddle. Incorporating lateral work with passage helps to engage the hindlegs and keeps the flexion and bend supple which, in turn, should improve the overall quality.

Piaffe and passage are inter-connected and, more often than not, ridden together via transitions. The one movement merges into the other, as the rider allows the collection in piaffe to be moved seamlessly forwards into passage, and vice versa. Horses often find the transition from passage to piaffe easier than vice versa, as this transition requires less strength.

The transitions from walk into piaffe or passage are more difficult for the horse, as the walk, while active and impulsive, lacks any spring so the transition requires confirmed engagement and strength.

Another tricky transition in the Grand Prix test is from passage into canter. To ensure that this is a smooth, clean transition, a useful exercise is to take a slight inner track after the turn and, before the canter, leg-yield for a couple of steps in passage to engage the hindleg, then take a slight shoulder-fore position and make the transition into canter.

Definition of Passage

Basically, passage is a transition from collection into extension but, by virtue of half-halts from the rider's seat, leg and rein aids, the forward energy is checked and converted into an upward, impulsive, cadenced trot. Generally speaking, the leg aids for passage are given slightly further back than for piaffe so that the horse is clear about which exercise is wanted. Again, some riders and horses find that using the leg aids diagonally works for them – as before, this is a matter of choice and efficiency.

An energetic passage requires maximum engagement of the hindquarters, keeping the rhythm of the trot, to create the forward thrust and a horizontal upper front leg, but with a slow enough tempo

Passage: power and strength – Grand Prix.

Passage: power and strength – Grand Prix continued.

to create and keep the cadence. The work on the piaffe should have created the engagement necessary for the passage, and the rider can then gradually allow the forward movement into passage to develop with a slight give of the rein. Correct passage happens, via collection, from forward movement and not by holding the horse back with the reins. However, the hindquarters are now required to propel the body forwards, and the flexion of the hindleg joints will not be the same as in the piaffe.

The FEI definition of passage states that: *'The height of the toe of the raised forefoot should be level with the middle of the cannon bone of the other supporting foreleg. The toe of the raised hindleg should be slightly above the fetlock joint of the other support hindleg.'*

This definition does not differ greatly from that of piaffe. The major differences between the two movements are the power and forwardness of passage, its cadenced energy and lift.

Anything more exaggerated than the above definition means that the croup will come up and the engagement is likely to be diminished. Horses often come croup high through tension and a lack of self-carriage. This is a sign that the horse is still learning to take weight behind, so the rider needs to give him sufficient time to develop more strength, thus freeing the shoulders, and keep the exercises at a level that allows this to happen over time.

Teaching Passage

In the beginning, the horse is likely to find that his balance in passage is difficult to maintain, so the rider should take him once more into piaffe, albeit briefly, and then allow the forward tendency again for just a very few strides of passage. Then it is best to allow the horse to move forwards into a normal trot to relax the muscles and the brain.

In the spirit of thinking outside the box, there are advocates of teaching Spanish walk to horses as a means to encourage the lifting and extending of the shoulders as a precursor to passage. This is a reasonably 'alternative' method and one that requires experience and dexterity from the trainer.

It is very important, however, that the horse has a firm grasp of piaffe before you think about teaching him to do this, and as a secondary note of caution, this is probably not something to attempt if the horse already has a less than clear four-beat walk.

Initially taught from the ground, it is then combined, from the saddle, with increasingly close transitions between it and trot until the lifting of the Spanish walk is incorporated into the suspension and lift of the passage. We have enlarged on this in the 'Work In-hand' chapter, but it is not for novices!

Passage is a matter of muscle strength, confidence and balance and will take some time to become fully developed.

What one wants to see in passage:

- True collection, engagement and throughness
- Sufficient flexion of the joints to create power and thrust
- Lifting of the shoulders
- Straightness
- Maintenance of rhythm and an even tempo
- Balance and strength
- Regular, even, impulsive strides
- A forward inclination
- A light contact with the poll the highest point

The Spanish walk: not for novices!

What one often sees:

- Stiffness and hollowness over the back
- Heaviness in the hand and leaning on the reins
- Behind the vertical
- Uneven steps behind, often with a double beat from one (the weaker) hindleg
- Shoulders not lifting or raising sufficiently
- Plaiting in front
- Swinging behind
- Hovering steps

Hubertus Schmidt has this to say: '... *that the horse is high in front, but this needs to be matched by a lowered croup for the correct balance. Very often the rider has not got the back, the front legs are high and nothing happens behind.*'

Any tension or fatigue will ensure that the horse becomes sore in his back due to restricted blood flow and oxygen distribution. Over-working these exercises will prove to be counter-productive, particularly with a younger, less strong horse. Strength in the hindquarters is developed by basic collection and extension exercises within trot and canter to better create impulsion and self-carriage.

Another important consideration is the straightness of the horse. A crooked horse will sway or swing the quarters as he lacks the physical strength to maintain the carrying power and remain balanced. If his straightness is in question, then the remedy, as is very often the case when training, is usually to take a step back to correct the problem, using lateral work, transitions and half-halts.

A hovering trot is not correct passage and should never be encouraged.

It is important to have clarity between the various trots, particularly with a horse coming into advanced level. A hovering trot does not have the necessary engagement and impulsion from behind and is a false friend.

These exercises need intelligent, progressive training in line with the horse's natural ability and balance so that he becomes familiar and confident in these most demanding of movements. Forcing a horse too early, and beyond his current self-carriage, when he is not mentally or physically able, ensures that problems will become ingrained.

It is as well to acknowledge that some horses will produce a better, more expressive passage than others because of their conformation and natural ability. Some have a good piaffe and a less good passage, and vice versa. The training should take such considerations into account.

The Finished Product

The top international horses can show piaffe, passage and transitions for nines and tens. These horses are often very hot and sharp so the rider's task is to keep unnecessary tension at bay and control everything, whilst keeping the lightness and suppleness that are ideally to be demonstrated.

In the end, the horse's willingness to perform piaffe and passage is fundamental to the quality of the exercise. Both horse and rider must have the focus, concentration and ability to present these movements. Whilst expression and lift within piaffe and passage are what makes the difference between ordinary and good movements, flashiness and unevenness are detrimental to the correctness of the exercises.

Successful training harnesses the horse's natural wish to please and his willingness to go forwards. The choice should always be to encourage these tendencies so that the horse finds the exercises almost playful. Resistance and tension are the enemies of correct work, and such exercises then become mechanical tricks.

The finished product should show impressive power allied with ease and harmony.

In the words of Klaus Balkenhol: *'The feeling is one of slow but majestic steps, that spring up and forwards.'*

15 Trainers/Coaches

The people who know the most about the work with horses aren't always the ones in charge.

Pat Parelli

Dressage is about education. Trainers/coaches are educators. Students and equines are learners. This applies to all ages and stages, and the threesome – horse, rider, trainer – all can, and should, learn from each other so that the education is three-way and ongoing.

The top trainers train all their horses and riders with Grand Prix in mind, quite regardless of the ultimate outcome, to ensure that the training is progressive and appropriate. Every top trainer has a 'method', gleaned from years of experience on lots of different horses, and also from watching and learning from other trainers and riders. Being open-minded and humble is essential to the successful riding and training of any horse, as each one reminds

Teaching/coaching: whatever the level, engagement between coach and student is essential.

us daily that there is still so much to learn whatever your age, stage and experience. No one ever knows everything. Ego is different from self-confidence and self-belief, and there is no place for ego in riding and training horses.

There is not just one 'right' method, as each horse will require an individual way of working and being worked. However, what is essential is to stick to the Scales of Training, which have evolved over many years, not to say centuries, from the knowledge and experience of first class horsemen and women, so that the end product is recognizably correct.

It can be challenging to find not just a good trainer, but one with whom you can form a working relationship, and who relates to you and your horse. It is important that you make a decision, before beginning the search for a trainer, about what it is that you want from the relationship. Do you want a professional to train and challenge you and your horse, or is it your preference for a more informal relationship, where comfort zones are adhered to, everyone has a pleasant time and all egos remain intact? Determine your own needs and priorities, and then choose accordingly.

Videoing a training session can be really helpful, and the best place from which to take such a video is in a corner (which is probably also where the trainer will mostly sit), as straightness, bend and positioning are easily seen. However, videoing a test is, ideally, filmed from A, as this is more or less what the judge sees, albeit in reverse, and so it is easier to evaluate the test and relate it to the test sheet. Watching these videos, preferably with your trainer, can be most valuable and instructive – but only if horse and rider are in the centre of the frame, or zoomed into as necessary, otherwise the pinprick on the horizon could be anyone, and you cannot make out what is happening! Good videoing is an art!

Finance also comes into the equation

– experienced Grand Prix trainers charge according to their hard-earned level of expertise and the years it has taken them to reach it. Training is their business. You would expect to pay a sensible amount for a top-level lawyer, doctor, professor, architect, veterinary surgeon, or other professional, and trainers need the same consideration. You are paying money to someone with greater expertise than you in a sport at which you would like to excel, so it makes sense to open your mind to what this person can teach you and your horse to achieve the best value for money.

Trainers tend, to become coach, counsellor, arbitrator (between you and your horse), technical adviser and psychologist, blurring the edges of what started out as a relatively simple amateur/ professional relationship. Not every trainer is good at every aspect, any more than every rider is good at riding every horse. This relationship, which can become quite intense, needs mutual respect and give and take from all parties.

Personal recommendation is always valuable, and attending higher level competitions to see riders and trainers at work can be most useful. Do bear in mind, however, that talented riders do not always make talented, or even good, trainers – you ideally need someone who has both strings to their bow. Equally, not all trainers have the wherewithal to compete themselves at the top levels, but they can still be excellent trainers. Ideally, however, he or she should be willing to ride your horse, when necessary or desirable, as this is a massive help in the learning curve for horse, rider and trainer.

From the ground, what is seen can be misleading and is no substitute for feel.

Modern thinking about training tends more towards coaching rather than just instructing. The latter is, however, necessary when someone is learning to ride because there is a need to be told what, why and how to do it. When the rider is more competent and advanced, coaching methods can come into play with great advantages all round. Riders are coached to find ways of riding and training that suit their learning preferences via questions and answers, by trying something out and then discussing the success or failure of their efforts. In this way, coaches guide and suggest rather than instruct and insist. Riders thus take more responsibility for their own riding and training, and in the process are less dependent on their trainer when they need to ride alone.

What is crucial is that the sessions are rider centred rather than trainer centred. The perspective and goals of the rider should be paramount without compromising the principles of training. The above applies whether or not you intend to compete – training is training, and competing is only one way of having your competence and level assessed by a third party.

In the UK and elsewhere in the world there are riders who will only train with a 'name'. The very top trainers are in huge demand, but they have equally huge demands on their time and are, more often than not, running a yard, giving clinics, dealing in horses and competing themselves, which means that they are not always available. It makes sense, therefore, to have a regular trainer to whom you can go as often as possible, and as often as you need, who will know you and your horse very well. By all means, also go to the 'name', but have regular, frequent back-up the rest of the time. It can also be most beneficial for your regular trainer to go with you to the 'name' so that all parties are 'in the loop'. 'I train with so and so' might sound impressive but if you only go to them a couple of times a year, the very best of them will struggle to take you forwards and upwards and, realistically, you do not really train with them!

On the above topic, be honest about your own level of expertise, the level of training at which you and your horse currently perform, and your ultimate aims. The top trainers will expect a certain level of competence from you so they can be of help, and so that you get your money's worth.

When you do find the right trainer, stay with them. Any trainer worth his salt is doing all he can to build his own knowledge, expertise and success for you and your horse. No one, whether rider, owner or trainer, ever knows it all – and there is seldom a point with horses and their training where further improvement is not possible.

However good you might think yourself to be, it is of the utmost importance that you get regular help from a good professional rider/trainer. Everyone needs 'eyes on the ground'. The top riders have their trainer/coach with them at all, or nearly all, their training sessions and at competitions. Practically and financially this is often beyond the majority of riders, but spend your money on what will actually help you to achieve your goals. What is definitely true is that money alone will not buy success: it never has, and it never will – but it does buy opportunities, so make the most of what is available to you.

It's unwise to pay too much, but it's worse to pay too little. When you pay too much, you lose a little money – that's all. When you pay too little, you sometimes lose everything, because the thing you bought was incapable of doing the thing it was bought to do. The common law of business balance prohibits paying a little and getting a lot – it can't be done. If you deal with the lowest bidder, it is well to add something for the risk you run, and if you do that you will have enough to pay for something better.

John Ruskin (1819–1900)

PS: Training is so much more important to progress than fashion. By all means have the latest gear, but make sure that your priorities are to improve yourself as a rider and train yourself and your horse to the best of your ability – then the smartest apparel will be appropriate!

Le Mieux trophy (Nationals 2014)...

...and the scoreboard at the 2012 Olympics.

16 Conclusions: Putting Everything Together

Success is the sum of small efforts, repeated day in and day out.
Robert Collier

The greatest mistake you can make in life is to be continually fearing you will make one.
Elbert Hubbard

Riding at advanced levels is about knowledge, patience, time, practical application, focus, concentration, determination – and hard work.

It can take days, weeks, months to teach one thing well to a horse, and then more time yet to consolidate that exercise – it is all too easy to hurry, and that can mean that you just get to something incorrect more quickly! The way of going and the quality of the paces are the essences of dressage and should remain paramount.

Movements done badly improve nothing and achieve nothing.

The desirable outcome is that everything you do is smooth, fluent, equal on both reins, easy and enjoyable. The last is relative – a demanding test or work session is probably only enjoyable when you have achieved it and finished – and then you and your horse might resemble the 'Happy Athletes' that the FEI promotes!

Much thought, time, effort, discussion and research have gone into the realization of this book; we thought it would probably be easier the second

time around – how wrong we were! Education is never complete, and we have learnt a huge amount. It is amazing how thorough one has to be when describing or explaining a movement or a feeling. We have been most fortunate to work with many talented, experienced people on the long journey of this book and we are most grateful to them for their time, care and effort.

Here are two nuggets of wisdom from Tim Stockdale (international show jumper), quoted recently (March 2015) in *Horse and Hound*: '*Good runs and bad runs have one thing in common, they don't last forever*' and '*Don't try so hard. Trying too hard to make things happen can mean you end up focusing on the negatives.*'

We really hope that you find this book useful, and that it helps you on your journey up dressage's long ladder.

If we can be of further help, or clarify something that is not as understandable as you would like, please feel free to get in touch via Angela's website – www. angelaniemeyereastwood.co.uk: we look forward to hearing from you!

And finally…

Light relief at the end! Sally Shetland (Sheepcote).

Appendix: The Talland and Sheepcote Horses, and Hayley Watson-Greaves

THE TALLAND HORSES

Abi Hutton on Amo.

Amo: Sixteen-year-old bay mare, Danish × TB: Amanti × That Talland Cat/Welton Louis. Inter II. Owned by Pammy Hutton and Lucile Webb Peploe.

Charlie Hutton on Pepe.

Super Blue (Pepe): Eleven-year-old bay gelding, Westfalian, Show Star × Florina/Florestan I. Inter II. Owned by Judy Peploe.

Abi on Sam.

Sail Away (Sam): Five-year-old dark bay gelding, Hannoverian. Novice level. Owned by Jackie Farlow.

Duela (Missy): Thirteen-year-old chesnut mare, Hanoverian, DiMaggio × Aquarelle/ Alabaster. Grand Prix. Owned by Pammy and Pippa Hutton and Phillip Woof.

Zidane VI (Danny): Eleven-year-old dark bay gelding, KWPN, El Caro × Hilda/Casanova. Medium level. Owned by Charlotte Dunkerton, leased by Abi Hutton.

Armagnac (Magnum): Ten-year-old bay gelding, Krack C × Temptation/Welt Hit II. Grand Prix. Owned by Pammy Hutton and Teresa Day.

Darius Hall (Darius): Seven-year-old black gelding, Hanoverian: Don Frederico × Kimberley/King Arthur. Medium level. Owned by Charlie Hutton and Jella Tupay.

Polly: Dark brown mare. Owned by Lizzie Hewison-Byrne.

TALLAND BIOGRAPHY

Talland School of Equitation, near Barnsley in Gloucestershire, is owned by Pammy and Brian Hutton, and run by them and their family: Charlie, Pippa, and their daughter-in-law, Abi.

Pammy's maternal grandmother, Mrs Ryder Richardson, founded the original school in Talland in Cornwall, hence the name. Pammy's parents, Lt Col and Mrs Sivewright, bought a rundown farm in Gloucestershire and over the years turned it into one of the foremost riding schools in the UK. Molly Sivewright and Talland had formidable reputations, and Pammy and her family have carried on the traditions and high standards started back in 1958.

Pammy, Charlie and Pippa are all international dressage riders who are entitled to wear the GB flag; Abi, Charlie's wife, rides for Ireland. Although dressage is the central focus at Talland, all spheres of equitation are catered for, including side saddle. The facilities of a top-end equitation centre are all in place: a massive indoor school, an even larger outdoor arena, stabling for 100, well kept and extensive turn-out, two cross-country courses, show jumps, a café, student accommodation, schoolmaster horses and several qualified instructors with many years of experience between them. See more on the website – www.Talland.net.

A career or a life with horses? Usually they are one and the same, the equine species tends to be extraordinarily time and interest consuming.
Molly Sivewright, *Thinking Riding*.

THE SHEEPCOTE HORSES

Sheepcote Don Calisto: Nine-year-old bay gelding by Don Schufro × Luckby Boy/Eufraat. PSG. The ride of Lucy Pincus at small tour.

Sheepcote Fiesta: Nine-year-old bay mare by Fuerst Heinrich × Siesta/Saluut. Working towards Grand Prix.

Sheepcote Let's Go: Five-year-old black gelding by Lord Loxley × Rubinstein/Wittelsbach. Young Horse classes and Novice.

Sheepcote Fantasia: Ten-year-old brown mare by Fairwell III (Federmark) × Don Primero/Lucky Boy. PSG. Ridden by Serena Pincus.

Sheepcote Whistle: Seventeen-year-old bay gelding by Wurlitzer × Siesta/Saluut. Grand Prix Schoolmaster.

Sheepcote Suncrest: Six-year-old bay gelding by Don Schufro × Lucky Boy/Eufraat. Medium level.

Sheepcote Chance: Ten-year-old bay gelding by Cassander × Rubinstein/Wittelsbach. Grand Prix. Ridden by Cherylee Cameron.

Donna of Sheepcote: Seven-year-old chestnut mare by Don Schufro × Woermann. Novice (working on advanced movements at home). Ridden by Paula Behrens.

Sally Shetland: Nine-year-old black mare.

SHEEPCOTE BIOGRAPHY

Sheepcote is the home of David, Serena and Lucy Pincus in rural Herefordshire. David started his riding career as a child, and was most fortunate to have classical training from former cavalry officers of the Russian School. His extensive experience, over many years, includes time at Crabbet Park in the UK, with help from Robert Hall and Pat Manning; at the HQ of German Equestrianism at

Serena Pincus on Sheepcote Fantasia.

Warendorf and also in Karlsruhe, with Herr von Neindorff; in Vienna training with the Spanish Riding School, where he received an offer of a job at the School; in France with the Cadre Noir at Saumur; in Germany at the Westphalen State Riding and Driving School; and a job with the late great German Olympian, Dr Reiner Klimke, in Muenster, riding the young horses and also the competition horses.

Along the way David gained a diploma in horse breeding from the Newmarket School of Stud Management and, in November 1980, he started Sheepcote Equestrian to carry out his primary objectives of training horses and riders for dressage, several of whom have ridden at World and Olympic competitions, alongside breeding dressage horses, for which he obtained further qualifications in modern stud techniques. David competed to international Grand Prix and has produced and ridden more than ten Grand Prix horses over the years, some of whom also perform the High School movements usually only seen at the Spanish Riding School.

Serena Pincus won several National Championship titles on her home-bred horses, and apart from training with David, she worked and trained in Germany with Margit Otto Crepin, a former European and Olympic Champion.

Lucy is a successful young rider currently on the Young Rider Squad (2015).

See more at www.sheepcote.com.

HAYLEY WATSON-GREAVES

WG Rubins Nite, eleven-year-old black gelding, by Rubin Royal out of a Limbo mare.

After a successful career with eventers and working hunter ponies, Hayley turned to dressage as a Junior rider. Now a Senior, she is based in Gloucestershire, and is a freelance rider/trainer with three of her own horses competing at Grand Prix; WG Rubins Nite is her international horse. Hayley is currently a member of the World Class Development Programme.

Bibliography

Bartels, T and J. *Ride Horses with Awareness and Feel* (J.A. Allen, 2008).

Eastwood, A.N. and Hessay, A.E. *Understanding Dressage Training* (The Crowood Press, 2011).

FEI Working Committee, *FEI Dressage Handbook; Guidelines for Judging* (Federation Equestre Internationale, 2007).

Hester, C and Ellison, P. *Real Life Dressage: Training Advice from Novice to Grand Prix* (Kenilworth Press, 2004).

Heuschmann, Dr G. *Tug of War: Classical versus 'Modern' Dressage* (Trafalgar Square Books, 2007).

Kottas-Heldenberg, Arthur, with Fitzpatrick, Andrew *Dressage Solutions: A Rider's Guide* (Kenilworth Press, 2014).

Kottas-Heldenberg, Arthur, with Rowbotham, Julie *Kottas on Dressage* (Kenilworth Press, 2010).

Kyrklund, K and Lemkow, J. *Dressage with Kyra* (Kenilworth Press, 1998).

Meyners, Dr E. *Aufwaerm-programm fuer Reiter* (Franckh-Kosmos Verlag, 2008).

Niggli, W.M. *Dressage – a Guideline for Riders and Judges* (J. A. Allen, 2003).

Podhajsky, A. *The Complete Training of Horse and Rider* (The Sportman's Press, 1991 – English translation).

Prockl, E. *Wenn Erwachsene in den Sattel Wollen* (Cadmos Verlag, 1998).

Schoeffmann, Britta *Klaus Balkenhol, Dressurausbildung nach klassischen Grundsaetzen* (Franckh-Kosmos, 2007).

Stahlecker, F. *Das Motivierte Dressurpferd: Die Hand-Sattel-Hand-Methode* (Franckh-Kosmos, 2000).

Tellington-Jones, L. *Getting in Touch with Horses* (Kenilworth Press, 1995).

Zettl, W. *Dressage in Harmony* (Half Halt Press Inc., 1998).

JOURNALS AND WEBSITES

British Dressage magazine (Think Publishing)

BD Rules, British Dressage

Dressage Online
www.dressagetrainingonline.com

Dressage Today magazine and online
www.dressagetoday.com

Eurodressage
Dr Astrid Appels, Belgium; www.eurodressage.
com

FEI Rules for Dressage (Federation Equestre
Internationale 2014/15)

Global Dressage Forum Reports (Andrea
Hessay)

Horse and Hound (Time Inc.Com)

Horse Hero website
www.horsehero.com

Reiter Revue (Germany) (Paul Parey
Zeitschriftenverlag)

Index

OTHER EQUESTRIAN TITLES FROM CROWOOD

ISBN 978 1 84797 427 3

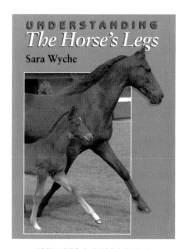

ISBN 978 1 86126 347 6

ISBN 978 1 84797 301 6

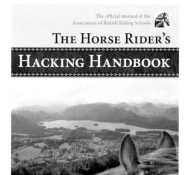

ISBN 978 1 84797 285 9

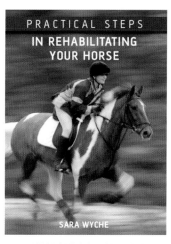

ISBN 978 1 84797 169 2

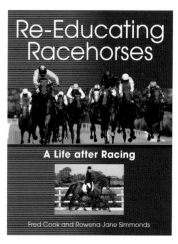

ISBN 978 1 84797 253 8

ISBN 978 1 84797 233 0

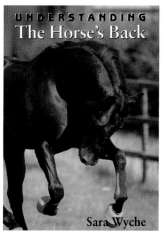

ISBN 978 1 86126 114 4

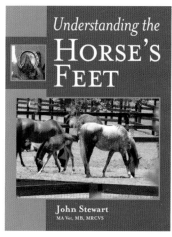

ISBN 978 1 84797 476 1